Saints Galore

Character Sketches for the New Calendar of Saints

by David L. Veal

Forward Movement Publications

It is very meet, right, and our bounden
duty, that we should at all times, and
in all places, give thanks unto thee,
O Lord, holy Father, almighty everlasting God. Who, in the multitude of
thy saints, hast compassed us about
with so great a cloud of witnesses that
we, rejoicing in their fellowship, may
run with patience the race that is set
before us, and, together with them, may
receive the crown of glory that fadeth
not away.

The Preface for All Saints' Day
The Book of Common Prayer

———

Second Edition

© 1989; © First Edition 1972, Forward Movement Publications,
412 Sycamore Street
Cincinnati, Ohio 45202

ISBN 0-88028-009-3

ALPHABETICAL LIST OF CONTENTS

i

Julia Chester Emery

Pioneer Enabler of Women's Ministries

On this day we celebrate the amazing ministry of an entire family, the children of a sea captain of Dorchester, Massachusetts. Two sons became priests. One daughter, Helen, cared for an invalid sister and maintained a household on 24th Street in New York City which became a famous place of refreshment for missionaries on leave. Another daughter, Mary, was National Secretary of the Episcopal Women's Auxiliary from 1872 until 1876. She was the visionary who dreamed the dream of what the Auxiliary could do in the foreign and domestic missionary field. And it was her sister, Julia, who through forty years of tedious and exhausting work, brought the dream to fruition.

Julia, whose day we celebrate, today, was National Secretary of the Women's Auxiliary from 1876 until 1916. She was a modest and self-effacing Victorian lady who was so careful to stay out of the limelight that it is difficult today to piece together all the things she did to advance the missionary efforts of the church and to enable women's ministries. She was a leader in the effort to get canonical status for our order of deaconesses. She invented and implemented the United Thank Offering. She was the indefatigable "Miss Julia" to a whole generation of missionaries, both men and women. Her entire life was focused on devotion to this one cause: the spread of Christ's kingdom.

1

William Laud

Archbishop of Canterbury

Died January 10, 1645

Anglican Martyr

William Laud was a humble tailor's son who proved his competence in the Church of England as a scholar and administrator and in 1633 was elected Archbishop of Canterbury. By then the church was seriously weakened by the controversies of the Reformation. Laud attempted to renew the power of the church and to restore its influence over the lives of men. As an advocate of "Uniformity" and the "Via Media" of the Church of England, he encountered violent opposition from various extremist groups. He made powerful enemies when he opposed the brutal practice of "enclosure."

Archbishop Laud was sincere, positive, quite self-less in his devotion to duty, and surprisingly tolerant for his time. He was tragically tactless and undiplomatic and sadly inept at reading public opinion. He was unable to stem the rising tide of Puritan political power in England. The most extreme militants gained control of the government and beheaded Laud on a trumped-up charge of treason. He died with the dignity and confidence of a Christian martyr. Indeed, he is often considered such. All of England was soon to learn how ruthless and tyranical the militant wing of the Puritan party could be.

The Prayer for Congress and the Prayer for the Church might serve as fruitful reading on his feast day since both are Laud's.

Aelred

Abbot of Rievaulx

An Exemplary Friend of God and Men

Aelred, son of a Christian priest of Hexham, England, through his skill at getting along with people became Master of the Household of the King of Scotland. His patience and firm but gentle bearing earned him both the love and respect of the court.

Many tears were shed when he left Scotland at the age of twenty-four to embrace the austere life of a Cistercian monk at Rievaulx in Yorkshire. There he pursued with rigor the friendship of Jesus Christ, gladly submitting to mortification and hard labor, to constant prayer, meditation and study. "This is the yoke," he said, "which does not crush but liberates the soul; this burden has wings, not weight."

Gracious and sensitive toward his fellow monks, Aelred became Abbot of Revesby in Lincolnshire and later Abbot of the great monastery at Rievaulx. There he presided over some three hundred monks. Under Aelred's leadership the community became a living model of peace and charity, a true colony of the kingdom of heaven. There he wrote his book, *On Spiritual Friendship,* warmly extolling the joy and strength of friendships, divine and human.

3

Hilary

Bishop of Poitiers

Pastor and Teacher in Gaul

Hilary was born of a powerful pagan family in Gaul. He became a Christian and, perhaps due to the prestige of his name, was elected Bishop of Poitiers as a young, married layman. He accepted the call, "with fear and trembling," and threw himself wholeheartedly into the task of shepherding his flock.

In his time many Christians in Gaul were Arians. That is, they accepted Jesus as "master and son of God," but denied that he was truly God. Hilary questioned the truth of such teaching and was soon exiled by Arian leaders of the church. He fled to the Eastern Mediterranean, then the heartland of Christianity, and there he learned theology and developed his pastoral skills. Tutored by the same Christian leaders who wrote the Nicene Creed, Hilary became a champion of the orthodox Christian faith. He not only returned to his diocese, but he eventually gained general acceptance there and exerted influence throughout Western Europe.

He was a tireless teacher. One of his famous pupils was Martin of Tours (see November 11). Hilary was largely responsible for the acceptance of the Nicene Creed in Western Europe. We honor him best when we seek a genuine understanding of Trinitarian doctrine.

Grant that we may hold fast to your servant Hilary's faith in Jesus Christ as Very God and Very Man.

Antony

Abbot in Egypt

Father of Christian Monasticism

Many young men of the third century world despaired of their decaying, materialistic, and licentious society. In Egypt many fled into the desert in protest and for their own soul's health. Sometimes their behavior became almost as bizarre and unbalanced as the behavior of those from whom they fled. This was not true of Antony.

Antony's quiet and well ordered life of devotion in the desert stood out in contrast both to the wickedness of the contemporary world and the eccentricities of some other hermits. He gave away all his possessions to the poor and thereby freed himself from the demands of property. Still, he found that he had to fight a seemingly endless battle against his personal passions and temptations. He helped fellow Christian hermits to organize their lives in meaningful patterns of prayer, work, and meditation.

His own solitude was frequently interrupted by his concern for the secular church and by requests for counseling. He was a friend to Athanasius (see May 2) and his orthodoxy was unquestionable. It has been said that, "Alone in the desert, Antony stood in the midst of mankind."

Grant that the same Spirit which enabled Antony to withstand the temptations of the world may so strengthen us.

5

Strong Fisherman and Apostle

The confession of the disciple Simon Peter, "Thou art the Christ, the Son of the living God," is a milestone in the Lord's ministry, in the founding of the church, and in the history of mankind. On Peter's confession of faith lay the foundation of a new world order.

Peter was a simple fisherman of Gallilee, rough and impetuous. Andrew, his brother, called him to follow Jesus. He soon grew very close and dear to the Lord and was one of the "inner circle" of Jesus' companions. He was quick-tempered and impulsive, given to bursts of enthusiasm and lulls of depression. At the Last Supper he swore he would die rather than forsake Jesus, but he soon denied him thrice.

Following the Resurrection, Peter emerged as leader of the more conservative disciples, strenuously opposing the baptism of Gentiles. However, after a very dramatic dream, he had a real change of heart (see February 4).

Peter eventually went to Rome where, with Paul, he founded the mother church of Western Europe. There, during the Neronian persecutions, he was crucified with his head down. The peculiar position was at his own request for he did not feel worthy to suffer in the same manner as his Lord.

Almighty Father, who inspired Simon Peter, first among the apostles, to confess Jesus as the Messiah and Son of the living God: Keep your Church steadfast upon the rock of this faith.

Wulfstan

Bishop of Worcester

Protector of the Poor and Oppressed

Most students of history are aware of the cruel treatment the native English (Anglo-Saxons) received from their Norman conquerors after 1066. Few know that practically their only effective defender was the English bishop, Wulfstan of Worcester.

Wulfstan was reared by devoted Christian parents and was educated in the church. He entered the priesthood and was soon elected Bishop of Worcester, a position which he declined, prefering to enter a monastery. Some twenty-five years later, in the troubled years just prior to the Norman Conquest, he was again elected to the same bishophric and then accepted the call.

Wulfstan continued to live in virtual poverty. He encouraged laymen to exercise their rights and responsibilities in governing the church. After the Conquest, he did not hesitate to confront the Norman King and the Norman archbishop, appealing to their consciences as Christians and speaking at great personal risk. He secured some rights for the English serfs against their Norman landlords and for English laymen against their Norman bishops. With the help of Archbishop Lanfranc, he succeeded in ending the loathsome practice of selling Englishmen as slaves in Ireland. Wulfstan spent most of his ministry taking the Gospel and the Sacraments to the poor and the oppressed, the English people whom he loved so much.

Fabian

Bishop and Martyr of Rome

Scholar and Leader

In 236 a virtually unknown Christian layman was elected Bishop of Rome. Countless legends have arisen to explain his surprising election. Besides being simply a layman and not a native of Rome, he seems to have carried no outstanding distinction as a scholar or leader. He turned out to be a first-rate bishop in this important diocese. He is reported to have been an efficient organizer and administrator. Not being particularly well trained himself, he corresponded with Origen, Cyprian, and other knowledgeable Christians of Eastern Europe.

For fourteen years he faithfully and effectively guided the church in Rome. He dispatched some of the first missionaries to Gaul. Things seemed to be "coming up roses" for the Roman Church. Then, without warning, a severe persecution of Christians was initiated by a new Emperor, Decius. Bishop Fabian was one of the first to die.

Fabian's life is a bold reminder of how the calls of God and man come upon us unexpectedly, "like a thief in the night." Fabian recognized his call and responded faithfully in his living and in his dying.

O Almighty God, who has called us to faith in you, and has surrounded us with so great a cloud of witnesses: Grant that we, encouraged by the good example of your servant Fabian, may persevere in running the race that is set before us.

8

Agnes

Martyr at Rome

Youthful Witness

Under orders from the Emperor Diocletian, in 304, the giant politico-military machine of the Roman Empire went to work to rid itself of the troublesome subversives called Christians. Many children were the innocent victims of this efficient blood purge. Agnes of Rome is a famous example.

She was reared a Christian and when the persecution began, although Agnes was but a young teenager, she wished to witness for the faith. A Roman official was attracted to her and might easily have saved her life. He offered her jewerly and many pleasant gifts if she would renounce the Lord and her parents and worship the Roman gods. Infatuated by the innocent girl, the official then attempted to seduce her. She resisted and he became enraged. He had her tortured and publicly stripped and abused. At the culmination of this hideous orgy she was killed with a sword.

The Roman world was stunned by the story of Agnes' suffering, much as our world was stunned by the *Diary of Anne Frank*. In the next generation, when Christianity was made legal, a shrine was erected in her honor in Rome, and the Song of Mary, the Magnificat (Luke 1:46f), was sung in thanksgiving for the witness of little Agnes. God had indeed "put down the mighty from their seat" and "exalted the humble and meek."

Grant that we may share her pure faith in you.

9

Vincent

Deacon of Saragossa and Martyr

Steadfast and Faithful

Vincent was a deacon in an early Christian church in Saragossa, Spain. He was a trusted friend and assistant of the bishop, Valerius. He was a very effective leader and therefore a "prize catch" for the Spanish Governor, Datian, who was implementing the Emperor Diocletian's policy of persecution. Datian's agents used every means known to them to "brainwash" Vincent, since, if he gave up Christianity, it would surely result in the defection of others.

Vincent was submitted to intensive argumentation, interrupted by excruciating tortures. He was beaten, chained, stretched on the rack, cooked on a gridiron, and the floor of his bare cell was covered with broken glass on which he had to walk and recline. Vincent did not renounce Christ or acknowledge the Roman deities.

Finally the exhausted and mutilated saint was released, perhaps as an example to other Christians of what they might have to suffer. He died shortly after his release. But his steadfastness, far from discouraging other Christians, strengthened them in their determination to remain faithful to the Lord.

Even as your holy Deacon and Martyr Vincent triumphed over suffering and despised death: Grant that we may endure hardness and wax valiant in fight.

Phillips Brooks

Died January 23, 1893

Bishop of Massachusetts

Renowned Preacher and Pastor

Although many know him only as the author of "O Little Town of Bethlehem," Phillips Brooks was probably the greatest American preacher of the nineteenth century. He was a native of Boston and was educated at Harvard University and the Virginia Seminary. He served two churches in Philadelphia and was for twenty-two years the rector of Trinity Church, Boston. He died less than two years after his election as Bishop of Massachusetts.

We have volumes of his sermons and they are certainly excellent, but reading them today one misses their most important ingredient, the warmth and strength of the person who composed and delivered them. He had a real gift for warming the hearts and stimulating the minds of his listeners. James Bryce wrote, "There was no sign of art about his preaching, no touch of self-consciousness. He spoke to his audience as a man might speak to his friend, pouring forth with swift, yet quiet and seldom impassioned, earnestness the thoughts and feelings of his singularly pure and lofty spirit." He preached sound Christian doctrine to listeners who ostensibly had no interest in such—and he got by with it! Although he was theologically quite orthodox and conservative, he came to be considered a "liberal" leader in his day simply because of his concern and interest in the social and intellectual issues of the times.

Timothy and Titus

Companions of Saint Paul

Both Timothy and Titus were gentiles, i.e. non-Jews, converted by Paul. Each seems to have accepted the Christian faith at the end of a long and deep personal struggle. It was not an easy step to take. Nor did the early church find it easy to accept a gentile into the "household of the faithful" (see February 4).

These men became close friends of Paul, and they accompanied him on several of his missionary journeys where they proved to be invaluable assistants, especially in the Greek cities of Corinth and Thessalonica.

From Paul's letter to Titus, which is contained in the New Testament, we assume that the Apostle left Titus on the island of Crete. Titus is believed to have been the chief organizer of the church on that island.

Paul frequently used Timothy as a "trouble-shooter" and "follow-up man" in his ministry. Timothy followed Paul to Rome and visited him in prison there, but escaped the Neronian persecution. Timothy spent his last days witnessing to Christ in Ephesus where, according to Eusebius, he was beaten to death by a mob of pagans among whom he had opposed the licentious festivities of the goddess Diana.

Almighty and merciful God, who called your servants Timothy and Titus to endure hardship for the sake of your dear Son: Strengthen us in like manner to stand firm in adversity.

12

John Chrysostom

Bishop of Constantinople

Great Preacher and Pastor

In an influential, prosperous, and sophisticated city at the apex of international power, it is rarely popular to advocate restraint, self-control, and responsible living. When the leaders of mighty Constantinople elected John Chrysostom to be Patriarch of the city they thought they had elected a "holy man" who would bless and affirm them in their way of living. They were only half right.

Bishop John's powerful sermons in the great cathedral, Santa (Hagia) Sophia, soon became a "cauldron of scalding water" thrown in the faces of the rich and proud citizens of Constantinople. His example of piety, charity, and simple living was an embarrassment to many. Eventually, through the intrigue of a vain and powerful lady, Eudoxia, and a jealous and corrupt clergyman, Theophilus, John was exiled. He died as a prisoner on a forced march into the Caucasus Mountains in winter, a martyr for righteousness in a society bent on lust. However, his preaching and exemplary living had so touched the hearts of many that sweeping reforms were soon instituted and life in the great city was profoundly changed for a generation or more.

The numerous volumes which we have of his sermons and commentaries have not lost their relevance today. The Liturgy of the Church in Constantinople, which he profoundly influenced, still bears his name. From this we get the "Prayer of St. Chrysostom" (Prayer Book, page 20).

Thomas Aquinas

Friar

Famous Theologian

Perhaps the greatest of the many medieval theologians, Thomas was the son of a prominent Italian count. He joined the Dominican Order against the will of his family. He studied at Monte Cassino and at the Universities of Naples, Cologne, and Paris, earning a Master's degree. Virtually his entire life was spent in teaching and writing.

His greatest work was the *Summa Theologica,* a masterful systematic statement of doctrine. It was by no means an immediate success, but time has proven it to be one of the finest intellectual expositions of the Christian faith ever composed. Some three centuries after his demise he was declared "Universal Teacher" to the church. He was particularly concerned about the relationship of faith and reason. He successfully reconciled the philosophy of Aristotle and Christian doctrine.

Thomas's intellectual genius was matched by a deep devotion to the Lord and by a rich spiritual and ethical life. He wrote many hymns, six of which appear in the *Hymnal 1940* (numbers 193, 194, 199, 200, 204, and 209).

O God, by whose Holy Spirit is given to one the word of wisdom, and to another the word of knowledge, and to another the word of faith: We praise your Name for the gifts of grace imparted to your servant Thomas, through whose teaching we know you better.

Abbess of Kildare

Mary of the Gael

Born out of wedlock on a sunny morning, Brigid's life and work brought light out of the darkness of early medieval Ireland, Scotland and Wales. She grew up a milkmaid and cowherd in bondage to the Druids. So many apocryphal fancies have been used to embellish her life story, that it is impossible to reconstruct an accurate biography. She was converted to Christianity and she did found a religious order which was mixed, men and women, after the fashion of the Celtic Church. Like Hilda of Whitby (see November 18) she served as abbess (female abbot) of this order in Kildare. Tradition has it that she was consecrated bishop in order to serve in this capacity. Such consecrations of females were not unheard of among the Celtic Christians of the British Isles.

She was renowned for her virtue, piety and charity and came to be so loved and honored among the Gaelic people that she was called "Mary of the Gael." Churches were named for her throughout the British Isles before the coming of the Anglo-Saxons and the Roman Catholic missionaries. A medieval hagiography of Lismore says of her, "She was abstinent, she was innocent, she was prayerful, she was patient, she was glad in God's commandments, she was firm, she was humble, she was forgiving ... she was a Temple of God. Her heart and mind were a Throne of Rest for the Holy Ghost."

Anskar

Archbishop of Hamburg

Missionary to Denmark and Sweden

This Saxon monk of Corbie, France, was one of the first Christian missionaries to the notorious Vikings. Most of the descendants of the Vikings are today's Danes, Swedes, and Norwegians. However, a significant Viking strain entered England through the Danelaw and the Norman Conquest.

Anskar established the first Christian school in Denmark, but was soon run out by local heathens. Undiscouraged, he moved on to Sweden where he founded that country's first Christian church in about 832. His interest in the Vikings did not wane when he accepted a call as bishop of Hamburg in Germany. He continued to initiate missions, especially in Sweden. It was not until long after his death that Sweden became a Christian country, but he had sown the seeds of her conversion, and it is for this reason that he is highly honored in Sweden to this day.

The Church of England has enjoyed centuries of happy relations with the Scandinavian churches, especially with the Church of Sweden. The Episcopal Church in America includes "Old Swedes" churches which were established by the Church of Sweden in colonial times. The feast of Anskar provides an appropriate occasion to thank God for the gift of brotherhood among Swedish, English, and American Christians.

O Lord, bless Anskar and the Scandanavian peoples.

Cornelius the Centurion

First Gentile Christian

Our Lord, of course, was Jewish. Some felt that the Christ had come to the Jews alone and that one must first become a Jew in order to become a Christian.

Cornelius was a Gentile and a centurion (an officer in the Roman Army) stationed at Caesarea. He was widely respected among the Jews, not only because of his important position but also because he gave liberally to the poor and "honored God as they did." He was called "upright and God-fearing." He learned of Jesus Christ from the Apostle Peter, received the Holy Spirit and was baptised.

It was Cornelius' profession of faith that led Peter to exclaim, "God has shown me that I should not call any man common or unclean. . . . God shows no partiality, but in every nation anyone who fears him and does what is right is acceptable to him." Perhaps the testimony of Cornelius would be helpful to those in our own time who see Christianity as a purely cultural or racial thing. He is a fitting patron for the career soldier.

O God, who by your Spirit did call Cornelius the Centurion to be the first Christian among the Gentiles: Grant to your Church in every nation a ready mind and will to proclaim your love to all who turn to you with unfeigned hope and faith; for the sake of Jesus Christ our Lord, who lives and reigns with you and the same Spirit ever, one God, world without end.

17

The Martyrs of Japan   *February 5, 1597*

A Community that Kept the Faith

Japan was first introduced to Christianity by Francis
Xavier, a great Roman Catholic missionary. For nearly
half a century the churches he founded flourished and
grew. Finally, the Japanese government became alarmed
at the spread of Christianity which they regarded as a
cloak for subversive activity by foreigners. Christianity
was made illegal, and to show that the authorities meant
business, twenty-six Japanese Christians were publicly
crucified in Nagasaki.

But this was only the beginning. For the next two
hundred and fifty years, if a Japanese were found to be
practicing Christianity he was subject to the death
penalty. Through the years many thousands died rather
than forsake Christ. At last the ban was lifted in 1859.
Christian missionaries again entered Japan (see Chan-
ning Moore Williams, December 2). To their astonishment they discovered several secret Christian communities still surviving, without priests and with very little
education, but still keeping the Faith in a most admir-
able manner, as they had through centuries of persecution.

*Almighty God, by whose grace and power your holy
martyrs in Japan triumphed over suffering, and were
faithful even to death: Grant us, who now remember
them in thanksgiving, to be so faithful in our witness to
you in this world, that we may receive with them the
crown of everlasting life.*

Absalom Jones

Died February 13, 1818

Priest

Courageous Black-American Pastor

Absalom Jones was reared a domestic slave on a plantation in Delaware. His charm, wit, and sincerity gained for him the affection of all who knew him. He was able to save enough pennies, given to him as tips, to purchase for himself a primer, a spelling book, and a New Testament. This was the beginning of an insatiable quest for knowledge which was to occupy much of his life.

When he was sixteen years old his mother, five brothers, and one sister were sold and he was taken to Philadelphia with his master. The more stimulating environment of the city, added to a desire to correspond with his mother, resulted in an intensified effort to learn. He went to night school and also studied theology under Bishop William White (see July 17) from whom he eventually received holy orders. He married, bought a house and land, and finally, at age thirty-seven, he was granted his freedom. Finding that Philadelphia's "white" churches were not truly open to him or his people, he founded St. Thomas Church for Americans of African descent.

He was an exemplary pastor and an able student of Holy Scripture and human nature. He had found the Good Master and in his Name had overcome seemingly insurmountable odds. He personified the indomitable spirit of his people who were one day to sing, "We shall overcome."

19

Cyril (Monk) and Methodius (Bishop)

February 14, 869 and 885

Missionaries to the Slavs

Apostles and Scholars

These brothers, Cyril and Methodius, were chiefly responsible for the conversion of the Slavic people of Eastern Europe in the ninth century. They were from Thessalonica, Greece. Each was educated at the great university at Constantinople, and each initially took up a career there; Cyril, the younger, as professor of philosophy and Methodius, the elder, as a librarian. Cyril was the first to do missionary work. He worked among the Tartars of what is now the Soviet Ukraine.

The brothers went together as missionaries to Moravia (part of modern Czechoslovakia). Cyril invented an alphabet for the Slavic tongues of that area. Together they translated the Liturgy and the Scriptures into Slavonic, the language of the people.

The task of converting these Slavs was not easy and was made even more difficult by the competitive spirit of the various Christian groups nearby. There was pressure from the Roman Church to impose the Latin language on the population and pressure from Germanic Christians to accept the Arian heresy. However, Cyril and Methodius did not allow partisan strife to interfere with their evangelistic work, and they eventually gained the admiration of all parties. Methodius was consecrated Archbishop of Sirmium in 869, with the blessing of both Rome and Orthodoxy. Cyril died in that same year.

Thomas Bray

Priest and Missionary

Humanitarian and Educator

The church in colonial America was often neglected and badly used by both Englishmen and Americans. But she found a great champion in Thomas Bray, the Bishop of London's "Commissary" to Maryland. Bray was an Oxford professor as well as a priest. He took very seriously the task of educating poor clergymen, laymen, and children. His understanding and concern for America's Indians and Negroes was far ahead of his time. He founded church libraries and schools in England and America, raised money for missionary endeavors, and influenced young English priests to try their vocations in America.

Bray fought long and hard to get an American bishop consecrated, but failed. He founded two of our church's most effective missionary organizations, the SPCK and the SPG (now USPG), both of which are still in operation after two and a half centuries of work the world over.

The deplorable condition of England's prisons was of grave concern to Thomas Bray. He organized Sunday "Beef and Beer" dinners in those prisons and went to Parliament with proposals for prison reform. It was Thomas Bray who first suggested to General Oglethorpe the idea of founding a humanitarian colony for the relief of honest debtors, but he died before seeing this, the Georgia colony, a reality. Few clergymen have taken more seriously our Lord's command, "Feed my sheep."

21

Martin Luther

Priest

The Great Reformer

The figure of Martin Luther towers above the history of the church in the 16th century like a colossus. He was a peasant-born monk and spent most of his life teaching biblical studies at the University of Wittenberg in what is today East Germany. His heroic opposition to rigid clericalism, to the sale of indulgences, to ignorance of the Bible, to the adoration of relics and to the corruption of the Papacy, assured him a significant place in the story of the church. His bold witness before the Imperial Diet at Worms, "Here I stand! I can do no other. God help me!", sounded the clarion keynote of the Reformation. His inspired translation of the Bible into German set a standard of excellence for generations.

He wrote many hymns, among them the powerful and ever-popular "A Mighty Fortress" (*Hymnal 1982* number 687). His *Short Catechism* provided a model for both Catholic and Protestant teachers and his influence on liturgical reform was profound and lasting. Luther's reforms were moderate compared to those of the Calvinists and Anabaptists, or compared to those of the Counter-Reformation. The resultant "Lutheranism" is much akin to Anglicanism. In fact, we are in full communion with the Lutheran churches of Sweden and Norway and enjoy a close relationship with the Evangelical Lutheran Church in America.

Polycarp

Died February 23, 156

Bishop and Martyr of Smyrna

A Man of Courage

Polycarp, Bishop of Smyrna in what is now called Turkey, did not seek martyrdom and did not encourage others to do so. When persecution broke out Polycarp made every honorable effort to protect his flock and himself. He even hid in the country but, eventually, the authorities found him.

Since Christians worshipped Jesus Christ, an "unauthorized god," and since they refused to worship the Roman gods or the "Divine Caesar," they were considered atheists and subversives. At a great public festival in the arena in Smyrna, Polycarp was presented to the governor amid cries of "Kill the atheist!" from the excited and unruly mob. The governor admonished Polycarp to swear by Caesar and to revile Christ and thereby save himself. The old bishop's famous reply was, "For eighty-six years I have been his servant and he has done me no wrong; how can I blaspheme my King who has saved me? . . . You pretend not to know who I am, let me tell you plainly, I am a Christian. If you want to learn the doctrine of Christianity, set a day and hear me." Polycarp was publicly burned to death.

The Christians in Smyrna who escaped death in this wave of persecution wrote a letter describing the execution of their great bishop and sent it to other churches. We still have this famous letter, "The Martyrdom of Polycarp."

23

George Herbert

Died February 27, 1633

Priest

Poet and Pastor

George Herbert was brilliant, wealthy, well-born, handsome, and a favorite of the King and Court. To the astonishment of a generation of prominent Englishmen, he abandoned a promising career in public life, took Holy Orders, and accepted a call to the humble parishes of Fugglestone and Bemerton. As he put it, "Methought I heard one calling, 'Child.' And I replied, 'My Lord.'"

In his short life (George Herbert was only forty when he died) he made a lasting contribution to the church's life. He wrote *A Priest to the Temple; or the Country Parson.* He wrote many excellent poems and hymns (see *The Hymnal 1940,* numbers 290 and 476). Most important of all, he left us a beautiful example of a small town pastor. It was in tiny Bemerton, and not at the mighty Court of St. James, that George Herbert found depth and meaning in life. At Bemerton he was able to witness for his Master in unselfish service to others. He had learned an age old lesson. "Nothing," he wrote, "is little in God's service."

O eternal Lord God, who holds all souls in life: We beseech you to shed forth upon your whole Church in paradise and on earth the bright beams of your light and thy peace; and grant that we, following the good examples of your servant George Herbert, and of all those who loved and served you here, may at the last enter with them into your unending joy.

David

Bishop of Menevia

Apostle to Wales

When the Roman legions were withdrawn in the fifth century a nightmare of chaos and terror closed in on isolated Britain. England fell into the hands of the heathen Angles, Saxons, and Jutes and it appeared that Christianity might disappear from the Islands altogether. Some Celtic Christians withdrew into Wales and David emerged as their most effective leader.

David was a monk of noble birth, well educated, and a famous teacher and preacher. We have little concrete historical data concerning him. Even his name (probably Dawi) seems to have been distorted with the passage of time. We do know that he founded several monastic communities in Wales, and that these served as places of refuge for the homeless, as centers for the spread of Christianity, and as bastions of learning, justice, and good order in a hostile environment. David was the abbot-bishop of the monastery at Menevia. He, and other hearty pioneer monks like him, kept the light of the gospel shining in a very dark and troubled time.

O Almighty God, who did choose your servant David to be an apostle to the people of Wales, to bring those who were wandering in darkness and error to the true light and knowledge of you: Grant us to walk in that same light.

Chad

Bishop of Lichfield

A Leader who Learned to Change

In the seventh century sweeping changes were being made in church administration and in the forms of worship to which British people were accustomed. Chad, who had been educated at the great Celtic monastery at Lindisfarne, was a spokesman for the opposition to these changes. At the Synod of Whitby he defended the Celtic forms of worship and Celtic church order. But the Synod decided in favor of the Roman ways of doing things. Chad gracefully accepted the decision of the Synod and helped enforce the observation of the new liturgy.

Later Chad was appointed Bishop of York by the King, following the custom of the day. Meanwhile, Wilfred had been made Bishop of York by the Archbishop of Canterbury and the Roman Pope. Chad accepted the church's new way of doing things and resigned in favor of Wilfred. The Archbishop of Canterbury was so thankful and so impressed with Chad's humility and devotion to duty that he made him Bishop of Lichfield. There Chad lived very simply, not even affording himself the luxury of a horse, and exerted a powerful influence for holiness and sound religious practice.

Grant to us, your humble servants, a like faith and power of love you enkindled as a flame in the heart of your servant Chad.

John and Charles Wesley

March 3, Died 1791, 1788

Priests

Eighteenth Century Evangelicals

John and Charles were raised together at the rectory in Epworth. They studied together at Oxford and together they were ordained into the ministry of the Church of England. Together they journeyed to America and served together as missionaries in Georgia for the Society for the Propagation of the Gospel. Together they led the great evangelical revival of the eighteenth century.

This movement attempted to foster among Christians a strong personal commitment to Jesus. Its leaders, such as John and Charles, preached and sang in the open fields, on street corners, and in the market places. They actively opposed slavery and drunkenness. John was the more impressive preacher, Charles the musician. (*The Hymnal 1940* contains eighteen of Charles' hymns.)

The Evangelical Movement led to the formation of several religious societies. The most famous of these was the "Methodist" Society, so-called for its strict and methodical practices. Some of these societies, especially in America, separated from the English Church. John and Charles Wesley, however, did not forsake the Church of England. Their feast day would seem an appropriate time to recommit ourselves to the spread of Christ's Kingdom among all classes of men.

Perpetua and her Companions

Martyrs of Carthage

The wealthy widow Perpetua, of Carthage, not only became a Christian but she opened her home to Christian worship. When this was discovered by the authorities, she and several of her friends were imprisoned. Perpetua's small child was cruelly taken from her. One of her prison companions, Felicitas, a slave girl, gave birth to a baby while in prison. The baby was taken from her, also, as in the case of Perpetua. However, to the great relief of all the incarcerated companions, the baby was secretly adopted by Christian parents.

The experiences of the companions in prison, including the dreams and visions of Perpetua, were recorded and remain one of our most valuable documents of early Christianity. The companions were sentenced to be thrown to wild beasts in the arena. Their last act together was to exchange the kiss of peace. They went joyfully and triumphantly to their fate, Perpetua calmly tidying her veil in the face of the hideous onslaught.

Almighty and everlasting God, with whom your meek ones go forth as the mighty: Grant us so to cherish the memory of thy blessed martyrs Perpetua and her companions, that we may share their pure and steadfast faith in you; through Jesus Christ our Lord.

Gregory

Bishop of Nyssa

Teacher of Christian Doctrine

At a time such as ours, when some persons take the spurious art of astrology so seriously, a Christian might well read this ancient Christian teacher's book on the subject, entitled *Against Fate*. This was one of many writings by Gregory against various forms of wrong thinking and wretched living.

Gregory was a brother of Basil the Great (see June 14) and served for many years as the Bishop of Nyssa in Cappadocia, a part of central Turkey today. He was a powerful preacher, a brilliant student of the Bible, and a deeply spiritual person. We still have a number of his sermons, biblical commentaries, and devotional and ascetical writings. Gregory attended the great Church Council at Constantinople in 381 and staunchly opposed the Arians. The Arians wrongly regarded Jesus Christ as only an agent of God rather than as the God-Man. Because of his convincing argumentation at this Council, Gregory came to be called the "Pillar of Orthodoxy." Through the years, his wise counsels and sound teachings led many into a fuller understanding of the Faith and saved many others from much unhappiness and error.

Enlighten by your Holy Spirit those who teach and those who learn, that, rejoicing in the knowledge of your truth, they may worship and serve you.

Gregory the Great
Bishop of Rome

Died March 12, 604

Renowned for Music

At a time when it looked as though England would be lost to heathenism forever, Gregory, Bishop of Rome, observed some handsome Anglo-Saxon lads being sold in the slave market and, moved with compassion, resolved to dispatch missionaries to England (see May 26). Within fifty years England was calling herself a Christian country and, furthermore, the Celtic Christians of the British Isles had been integrated into the Roman Church.

Gregory was no ordinary bishop! He was a patrician, a senator's son, and he had served as "mayor" of the city for some time before he decided to enter a monastery. Even after becoming a monk he served in a semi-governmental position as representative of the Bishop of Rome in the Imperial Capital, Constantinople.

It was in the year 590 that Gregory was elected bishop. He proved to be one of the most talented and effective bishops of history and, fortunately, he left us an excellent book on the subject, entitled *Pastoral Care*. He coined the title "Servant of the Servants of God" for his office. With virtually no help from the Imperial government he gained a lasting peace in war-torn Italy, and he organized the church in Western Europe to withstand the assaults of the Germanic and Viking invasions. He encouraged and contributed to a form of music which still bears his name, Gregorian Chant.

Patrick

Bishop and Missionary

Apostle to Ireland

Scarcely any saint has been as celebrated as Patrick.
Few have been more deserving. He was born of Christian parents in Roman Britain. At sixteen he was captured by barbarian raiders and carried off to Ireland as
a slave. After six years as a swineherd he escaped and
eventually returned to Britain. To the astonishment of
family and friends, he resolved to return to Ireland as a
missionary, and he began a long period of intensive
training in France. After many hardships and disappointments he was able to return to the land of his
bondage as a missionary bishop.

Patrick was not the first Christian missionary to Ireland but he was by far the most successful. Patrick
himself has left us a record of his experiences in his
Confessions—how he confronted the fierce King at Tara
and how he confounded the proud Druids. His sound
and effective teaching is reflected in a hymn, "I bind
unto myself today" (see *The Hymnal 1940*, number
268).

Most of Patrick's work was done in the northern part
of the island. His headquarters were at Armagh. He
made a famous pilgrimage into the mountains of Mayo.
He died at Saul in Ulster. It is said that he found a
heathen Ireland but left a Christian one.

*Bless your servant Patrick, O Lord, and all the people of
Ireland.*

Cyril

Bishop of Jerusalem

Great Teacher and Pastor

When famine hit the vicinity of Jerusalem, Cyril, the bishop, promptly sold some of the church's most prized possessions to relieve the poor and to obtain food for the starving. When the famine was over some angry church members succeeded in having Cyril condemned at a public meeting as an irresponsible thief who had illegally disposed of church property. They temporarily drove him out of the city. Although Cyril was a gentle and conciliatory man, this event was typical of the bitter controversy which racked his episcopate.

Scarcely had he regained his diocese before he was again expelled. This time by Arian heretics who had gained great power in Jerusalem. He was restored to the Jerusalem bishophric again by none other than the infamous Emperor Julian, the Apostate. Due to this rather coincidental fact, Cyril had difficulty regaining the confidence of the other orthodox bishops of the church. Furthermore, the Jerusalem Church had become notorious throughout the Christian world for its low moral standards. This situation Cyril attempted to correct, but his enemies blamed him for it.

Cyril's greatest talent seems to have been as a teacher and preacher. Very little of his thought was ever written down, but what we have is most impressive and timely even today.

Joseph

Foster-father of Jesus

In the face of circumstance that might have distressed a man of less stature, Joseph graciously assumed the role of Jesus' father. He is well remembered in Christian tradition for the love he showed to the boy Jesus who lived "under his roof" for at least twelve years. Joseph's tender affection and care for Mary has, likewise, been long celebrated in the church.

Joseph was a pious Jew, a descendant of David. He was a carpenter by trade, a man of very modest means, with no education outside the synagogue. It is generally believed that he died quietly and naturally, prior to our Lord's active ministry. The gospel writers tell us that Jesus was widely known as the "son of Joseph the carpenter," and Joseph's influence on him was, of course, inestimable. Jesus could not have had anyone less in mind than Joseph when he called God "father." Yet Joseph could not have had more than a vague inkling of the importance of his humble life. His life is a testimony to the value of simple everyday human things, especially that human thing called "fatherhood."

O God, who did call blessed Joseph to be the faithful guardian of your only-begotten Son, and the spouse of his virgin Mother: Give us grace to follow his example in constant worship of you and obedience to your commands, that our homes may be sanctified by your presence, and our children nurtured in your fear and love; through the same Jesus Christ our Lord.

33

Cuthbert

Bishop of Lindisfarne

Apostle to Northumbria

A man of large stature and unusual physical prowess, Cuthbert seemed destined from his youth for leadership. He, however, was always concerned that his spiritual leadership match his physical endowments. Prior to accepting a call to become Bishop of Lindisfarne, he spent eight years in prayer and meditation on the cold and isolated island of Farne.

Cuthbert's episcopate was brief but highly significant. It was occasioned by plague, war, and schism. He spent much time caring for and healing the sick and preaching against the superstitious use of charms and amulets. In the midst of war Bishop Cuthbert went fearlessly among his people, ministering to the wounded and inspiring hope in the survivors. He worked toward the reconciliation of those Celtic Christians who were dissatisfied with the liturgical and political changes being effected by the Roman Church in Britain.

Cuthbert led many men to salvation in Christ and contributed significantly to the Christianization of the North Country of England. Yet, holy living to Cuthbert meant a life of service. As the historian Bede put it, "He was aflame with the fire of divine charity; and to give counsel and help to the weak he considered equal to an act of prayer—knowing that he who said, 'Thou shalt love the Lord thy God' also said, 'Thou shalt love thy neighbor.' "

34

Thomas Ken

Died March 21, 1711

Bishop of Bath and Wells

A Symbol of Constancy

Most Americans are familiar with the Doxology, "Praise God from whom all blessings flow" (*The Hymnal 1940*, number 139), but few will recognize the name of its author, Thomas Ken. He was one of those rare souls who steered a straight course through the troubled waters of seventeenth century England.

Defending the "Via Media," he boldly defied three kings: James II, whose edicts Ken refused to read in church; Charles II, whose marital infidelity he condemned; and William of Orange, whose legal right to the throne he denied. This last protestation cost Ken his diocese. After more than ten years of wandering about jobless and homeless, he was finally reconciled to the Church of England under Queen Anne. He was then too old and infirm to resume the work of a bishop.

Thomas Ken was a masterful teacher, hymn writer, and pastor. He always lived very simply and he never married. The words of his will are a classic statement of his faith. "I die in the Holy, Catholic, and Apostolic Faith, professed by the whole Church, before the disunion of East and West: more particularly I die in the communion of the Church of England, as it stands distinguished from all Papal and Puritan Innovations."

O God, we give you thanks for the purity and strength with which you did endow your servant Thomas Ken.

35

James De Koven

Priest

Defender of Our Catholic Heritage

Success in the world's terms is not a usual reward for great and good men. James De Koven was certainly one of the greatest and best leaders of the Episcopal Church in the nineteenth century, yet his advice was rarely heeded. He was never made a bishop. The college he so carefully fathered no longer exists.

He was closely associated with the unpopular Ritualist party in a time when the church's life was especially marred by partisan strife. He succeeded in getting the General Convention to accept the fact that the viewpoints of the ritualists were at least not subversive. Through his reasoned and compelling oratory in defense of the catholic heritage, he enabled the church to stand above the petty sectarianism of the day and reaffirm its comprehensive nature. Perhaps his greatest achievement was in preventing the Episcopal Church from adopting a rigid, doctrinaire, and exclusive confession, after the manner of Protestantism.

James De Koven was a scholar and one of the really fine Christian educators of his day. He was a graduate of Columbia and of the General Theological Seminary in New York. He was a professor at Nashotah House and Warden of Racine College in Wisconsin for twenty years. He was an excellent pastor and a man "continuous in prayer."

Gregory the Illuminator *Died March 23, c.332*

Bishop and Missionary

Apostle to Armenia

The first Christian kingdom in history was Armenia, now a part of the Soviet Union. Armenia was converted through the efforts of Gregory. This kingdom came to an unhappy end as an independent state in A.D. 430, yet some two and one-half million persons today are still culturally Armenians. They enjoy a racial, linguistic, and religious heritage which is one of the world's oldest and richest. Their community has endured fifteen-hundred years of dispersion, harassment, and often severe persecution.

The truly marvelous story of Christian Armenia began when the infant Gregory, who was a prince by birth, was exiled by enemies and reared by a compassionate Christian family in Cappadocia (modern central Turkey). As an adult and a Christian he returned to Armenia and converted the King, Tiridates, heir of Gregory's old enemies. This was not done easily. Indeed, many legends have grown up around the tradition of Gregory's great difficulties, hardships, and sufferings in effecting the conversion of the king and subsequently the kingdom. For this work he is called the "illuminator." Gregory was eventually consecrated Bishop of Etchmiadzin and was the organizer of the Armenian Church.

The Episcopal Church has enjoyed a warm and friendly relationship with the Armenian Church for many years. Offer thanks for that friendship.

Charles Henry Brent

Died March 27, 1929

Bishop of the Philippines

Missionary Extra-ordinary

In 1902 a ship entered the port of Manila bearing the American Governor, William H. Taft, and the Missionary Bishop of the Philippines, Charles H. Brent. Bishop Brent arrived with all the trappings and prestige of the new American establishment. However, he soon demonstrated that he was going to resist the temptations that ruined many protestant missions. He refused to waste time criticising Roman Catholicism, the religion of most of the Filipinos, or to conduct a "chapel of ease" for the rich and comfortable American Episcopalians in Manila. He determined, instead, to go to the thousands of non-Christians on the Islands and also to see that the American rule in the Islands was responsible and ethical.

Bishop Brent founded several schools and an excellent charity hospital in Manila. He became a key opponent of the deadly opium trade in the Islands. He conducted a successful mission to the sophisticated Chinese of Manila and converted the pagan and uncivilized Igorots of Luzon. He dared to venture, unarmed, into the territory of the hostile Moros of the Sulu Archigelago, among whom he initiated a Christian mission. By 1917 his health was broken and he accepted election to the Diocese of Western New York, where he became an important leader in the new ecumenical movement. Everywhere he had served as a bold witness to Christ's love for "all sorts and conditions of men."

John Keble
Priest

Shepherd of the Oxford Movement

On July 14, 1833, before a distinguished group of judges assembled in the Church of St. Mary the Virgin, Oxford, John Keble preached a startling sermon entitled "National Apostasy." He accused the English government of forsaking its ancient and sacred commitment to Christ and his church. This sermon marked the beginning of the "Oxford" or "Tractarian" Movement which shook the English church and nation to its roots.

The movement aimed at rescuing the institutional church from rampant "liberalizing" reforms which threatened to render the church impotent. Renewed emphasis was placed on the idea of the church as a divine institution, on the historic episcopate, and on the Book of Common Prayer.

Of the many eminent churchmen who took part in this movement, John Keble was perhaps the most mature and certainly one of the best loved. His unquestioned loyalty to the Church of England, his wise and gentle leadership, held the movement together and prevented many defections from Christianity on the one hand and to the Roman Church on the other. In the face of bitter controversy, there was no guile found in him.

His religious poetry had such a fresh, simple, and straight-forward quality about it that it remains popular today (see *The Hymnal 1940*, numbers 155, 166).

39

John Donne

Priest

Poet and Preacher

"No man is an island. . . ." These oft-quoted words from John Donne are not only a terse statement of a universal truth, they point to a perplexing dilemma in this great man's life. How could John Donne be reconciled to the baffling world in which he lived; an age struggling with change, shattered by "the new learning," "the new art," "the new science," "the new government," and even "the new religion"? He felt deeply his own responsibility to deal with these changes. He refused to retreat to an "island."

Donne went through a troubled and reckless youth, characterized by cavalier gaiety on the one hand and by deep-seated anxiety on the other. His elegant poetry and the brilliance of his personality gained him many influential friends, but little success otherwise. He married, but could hardly be said to have "settled down." His charming wife bore him lovely children, but peace and satisfaction did not enter his life until he took his life to the Master.

Finally, he plunged himself into the church's life with all the fervour of his cavalier days. He was ordained and, after serving as a royal chaplain and as rector of Sevenoaks, he became Dean of St. Paul's, London. There he preached many celebrated sermons. His hearers were astonished and many of their lives were profoundly changed. His works have continued to stimulate thinkers and writers into our own time.

Frederick Denison Maurice   *Died April 1, 1912*
Priest

Theologian and Social Reformer

In 1848 virtually all of Europe was aflame with revolution. Governments were violently overthrown in France, Germany, and Austria. The Establishment in England shuddered and reacted rather fearfully. At least one Christian theologian, F. D. Maurice, responded positively and set to work to apply Christian principles in the acute area of social reform.

Maurice, along with John Ludlow and Charles Kingsley, organized the Christian Socialists. They publicized the use of Christian attitudes in solving social problems. They helped organize trade unions and promoted reform legislation. Their ideas and actions were unpopular with certain persons of the Establishment and Maurice was forced to resign his post in theology at King's College.

Undeterred, Maurice founded a Workingmen's College in London and pioneered in the field of education for working class people. He wrote and published many volumes, the most famous of which was entitled *The Kingdom of Christ*.

Maurice laid the groundwork for much modern English theology. He forged contacts between the church and the reforming movements in the state and thereby helped prevent in England the antagonism which typyfied church-state relations in some countries as these reforming groups began to take the reins of government.

41

James Lloyd Breck

Priest

Pioneer Missionary and Educator

James Breck was a pioneer in several ways. He was a pioneer in the revival of monasticism in our church. He was a pioneer missionary to the Old Northwest and to California. He was a pioneer in theological education, being instrumental in the founding of both Nashotah House and Seabury theological seminaries.

Breck was a native of Philadelphia and a graduate of the University of Pennsylvania and the General Seminary in New York. He joined two classmates in forming an experimental religious community under the direction of Bishop Kemper (see May 24) in the great wilderness of Wisconsin. There he lived in utmost simplicity and spent virtually every waking hour in religious work.

Indefatigable, Breck founded numerous churches, missions, and schools. He prayed, taught, traveled, and worked tirelessly to initiate and keep going the work of the church. Himself an ardent Anglo-Catholic, Breck rejoiced in the renewed emphasis on catholic doctrine and worship in his day. He preached and exemplified the extension of Christian discipline into every aspect of living.

In later years, with the church firmly established in Wisconsin and Minnesota, James Breck sought sunnier climes. He went to California and vanished into legend, a veritable "Johnny Appleseed" of the church.

Thank you for your servant James, indefatigable founder.

Richard

Bishop of Chichester

A Most Compassionate Scholar

Richard of Chichester was a tireless student of theology, a man constant in devotion to the Lord, and one whose life was filled with unselfish service to his fellowmen.

Although he was born to a prosperous family, Richard was orphaned at an early age and soon impoverished by a negligent guardian. He entered Oxford unable to afford even a gown or a fire in winter. Yet he did very well in his studies and was eventually able to go on to further study at the University of Paris and at Bologna.

He returned to England as a small-town parson, a role he always loved. However, his fame as a counselor and preacher soon spread far and wide. Against the wishes of King Henry III, Richard was consecrated Bishop of Chichester. The king denied him access to the cathedral and to the bishop's palace, so Richard spent two years wandering barefoot through his diocese, living very simply on the charity of his flock.

When the quarrel with the king was finally settled and Richard moved into the palace, he lived there almost as a beggar, wearing a hair shirt, fasting often, and sleeping on the floor. He was an efficient administrator and a stern disciplinarian when the occasion called for it. Yet he entertained the poor lavishly and ultimately willed his episcopal estate to the poor, to hospitals, to widows and orphans.

See hymn 429, *The Hymnal 1940,* by Richard of Chichester.

Martin Luther King Jr. *Died April 4, 1968*

Prophet of Justice and Peace

Civil rights leader, Nobel laureate for peace and Baptist clergyman, Martin Luther King Jr. was a dreamer of dreams. His ministry was based on a vision of human dignity for all people, an America free from racial prejudice, segregation and hatred. Martin Luther King was assassinated in Memphis, Tennessee, supporting striking black sanitation workers. His life and work were committed to securing equal rights for the poor and the dispossessed.

After receiving a Ph.D. degree from Boston University School of Theology, King returned to the South as pastor of a church in Montgomery, Alabama. It was in Montgomery, after organizing a boycott which led to the Supreme Court decision banning segregation on public transportation, that he was thrust into leadership of the civil rights movement. For the next twelve years King led demonstrations, marches and sit-ins protesting the evils of segregation and racism.

King's peaceful acts of civil disobedience led to jailings and brutal retaliation by whites. Despite physical threats and personal slander, King and his followers continued to awaken the conscience of the nation with their message of justice, equality and nonviolence.

King's most memorable speech, "I Have A Dream," delivered to 200,000 people during the March in Washington D.C. on April 28, 1963, reaffirmed his faith in the brotherhood of mankind.

(Contributed by Michael P.G.G. Randolph)

William Augustus Muhlenberg

Priest

Pastor and Humanitarian

The personality and character of this man captured the imagination of the entire Episcopal Church in the nineteenth century. He was claimed by all parties, calling himself an "Evangelical Catholic." He was an enthusiastic exponent of Maurice's ideas of Christian social involvement (see April 1). He was remarkably versatile, an excellent preacher, schoolmaster, and poet (see *The Hymnal 1940,* number 15).

For over forty years he served parishes in Pennsylvania and New York and became one of the most widely loved and trusted pastors of his day. Some consider the founding of St. Lukes Hospital in New York City his greatest achievement. However, he also founded two religious communities and a number of schools and contributed to the organization of several public charities.

Muhlenberg long exercised an important influence in the General Convention and the activities of the National Church. He was the chief author of the "Muhlenberg Memorial," a document which profoundly affected the life of the Episcopal Church. He was instrumental in initiating significant Prayer Book and Hymnal revision. In proposing his name for the Church's Calendar the Standing Liturgical Commission declared, "There was not a significant area of the church's life that he did not elevate and strengthen."

William Law

Priest

Renowned Pastor and Author

"If we are to follow Christ, it must be in our common way of spending every day." So wrote William Law in *A Serious Call to the Devout and Holy Life*. This quiet schoolmaster of Putney, England, could hardly be considered a revolutionary, yet his book had near revolutionary repercussions. His challenge to take Christian living very seriously received more enthusiastic response than he could have imagined, especially in the lives of William Carey, Henry Venn, George Whitefield, and the Wesley brothers, all of whom he strongly influenced. More than any other man, William Law lay the foundation for the religious revival of the eighteenth century, the Evangelical Movement in England, and the Great Awakening in America.

William Law came to typify the devout parson in the eyes of many. His life was characterized by simplicity, devotion, and the pursuits of charity. Because he was a Non-Juror he was deprived of the usual means of making a living as a clergyman in the Church of England. He therefore worked as a tutor (in the famous Gibbon household) and as a sort of "free-lance" minister. He organized schools and homes for poor children. He stoutly defended the sacraments and the scriptures against the flagrant attacks of the Deists. He spoke out eloquently against the ghastly warfare of his day. His richly inspired sermons and writings have gained him a permanent place in Christian literature.

George Augustus Selwyn
Died April 12, 1878

Bishop

Missionary to New Zealand and Melanesia

The first Bishop of New Zealand was trained at Eton and Cambridge and had credentials, talent, and influence enough to have lived a most comfortable and successful life in England. Instead, he chose to go half way around the world and live for nearly two decades under the most trying circumstances, forging the foundations of a new branch of the church in a most troubled land. It is exhausting even to read of his journeys through the islands of Melanesia and New Zealand, using the unsophisticated and sometimes hazardous nineteenth century modes of transport in an often hostile land.

Bishop Selwyn was a tireless evangelist, pastor, teacher, organizer, and administrator. Perhaps most important of all he gained the respect, indeed the love, of the native Maoris to whom he first brought the light of the gospel. During a decade of cruel and tragic warfare between the English colonists and the Maoris, he was able to bring the ministrations of Christ to both sides. Finally, he was able to play a reconciling role in the establishment of peace.

He was elected Bishop of Lichfield, England, in 1868 and held that office for the last ten years of his life. He was a capable scholar and a man of many interests, exercising influence in both the church and state.

We thank you for your servant George and his ministry in New Zealand.

Alphege

Archbishop of Canterbury

Martyr and Witness to the Danes

"From the wrath of the Northmen, Good Lord, deliver us." So prayed the English monks, but their prayer seemed of no avail. In 1011 Canterbury itself was besieged and taken by the fierce Danish Vikings. They carried the Archbishop, Alphege, off in their ships and demanded a ransom.

Alphege was an old and kindly monk from Deerhurst and later Abbot of Bath. He had been elected Bishop of Winchester under Dunstan (see May 19). For five years he had served as one of the most beloved and effective Archbishops ever to hold the See of Canterbury. He played a part in the conversion of King Olaf of Norway. Now Alphege was harshly bound, half-starved, and shamefully abused.

Englishmen immediately began raising the ransom, but Alphege, knowing how impoverished his people were already, refused to permit it. The enraged Vikings, in a drunken frenzy, fell upon the old Archbishop and savagely beat him to death. Yet, a number of them had been so impressed with the faith and compassion of their prisoner that they soon presented themselves for baptism.

Grant us, in like manner to your servant Alphege, constancy in faith and truth, and to fear none of the world's adversaries.

Anselm

Died April 21, 1109

Archbishop of Canterbury

Doctor of the Church

Anselm lived in an age when ignorance and raw power often went hand in hand. His life was spent in opposing these enslaving forces, especially in England.

He was born of noble Christian parents in Burgundy and educated at the monasteries at St. Leger and Bec in Normandy. He joined the latter community and, after an impressive career as teacher and author, became its abbot. He first visited England at the invitation of William the Conqueror, by whom he was well loved. His consecration as Archbishop of Canterbury met with overwhelming approval from the English people, who knew him as a wise and compassionate person.

He spent years in this high office attempting to gain a lasting peace in a time of constant feuding. He championed the church's independence from royal authority and was twice exiled by angry kings whose bidding he refused to do.

Anselm was a theologian of the first order. He lectured in Rome, carried on intellectual correspondence with the most brilliant leaders of his day, and wrote a number of books that are still highly regarded among theologians. His most famous book, *Cur Deus Homo?* was the foremost work on the doctrine of the atonement to come out of the Middle Ages.

O God, continue to enlighten us by the teaching of your servant Anselm.

Catherine of Sienna

Died April 29, 1380

Mystic and Humanitarian

One tends to think of medieval women as silent and passive dwellers in homes and convents. This was far from the case with Catherine of Sienna. She exercised great influence in matters of church and state and her's was one of the keenest minds of her day.

Her father was a merchant in the flourishing Italian town of Sienna. In her youth she had some extraordinary religious experiences which caused concern among her family and friends. At sixteen she joined the Third Order of St. Dominic and gave herself entirely to contemplation and the service of the sick and poor. Her reputation as a counselor and mystic soon spread far and wide. In 1376 she made a journey to Avignon and boldly confronted Pope Gregory XI who heeded her advice and thus averted schism and bloodshed.

Catherine's famous book, the *Dialogue,* is most unusual and highly symbolic. We have four hundred letters written by her, addressed to bishops, kings, scholars, merchants, and obscure peasants. They are excellent literature and reflect a wide range of interests.

Catherine spent countless months caring for the victims of plague. Again and again she was to be found in the courts of state, interceding for justice, mercy, and peace.

Deliver us, we pray, from an inordinate love of this world, that, following the example of your servant Catherine, we may serve you with singleness of heart.

Athanasius

Bishop of Alexandria

Died May 2, 373

Most Orthodox Theologian

"Athanasius Contra Mundum"—Athanasius against the world. In this phrase Christians have for centuries summed up the great life and work of this wise Bishop of Alexandria, Egypt. Long ago he became a symbol of orthodoxy, of right and clear thinking in the face of overwhelming opposition.

His thinking was ahead of his time. As Christians came to know and understand his teaching they came to feel that he offered the most accurate intellectual expression of their faith. The doctrine he espoused eventually became the universal teaching of the church and embodied in the creeds, especially the one that bears his name, the Athanasian Creed.

This did not come easily. For a time it seemed that, indeed, the whole world was against Athanasius. His chief opponents, the Arians, gained control of the church. He was deposed and exiled and vilified. He died without seeing the victory of his position proclaimed at the General Council at Constantinople in 381.

Basically, he opposed the Arian teaching that Jesus Christ was less than God but more than man. He held that such a being would be of no benefit to either God or man and could not reconcile God and man. Athanasius taught that Jesus Christ was truly God and truly man. In his renowned treatise, *De Incarnatione,* he wrote that God the Son "became as we are in order that we might become as he is."

51

Monnica

Mother of Augustine of Hippo

Monnica, the mother of Augustine (see August 28) has long been regarded as a paragon of Christian motherhood. She was certainly a very loving and loyal wife and mother. The portrait we have of her in Augustine's writings is more than most Christian mothers dream of.

In more recent times some other aspects of her character have come into focus. Thanks to the Freudian psychologists and the Women's Liberation movement, we can now view her in a new light. Considering Augustine's strong personality and virile interests she appears to have been at least an "adequate" mother. She had to struggle with a drinking problem of her own as well as with her husband's infidelity and violent temper. She was a very active participant in the "revolutionary" Christian movement. She was, of course, very much dedicated to her role as wife and mother, but she could hardly be called a "passive domestic." She was a most positive influence in her son's life, perhaps because she "led a life of her own." If one sees in motherhood constancy, affection, unselfishness, patience, wisdom, and integrity, then Monnica is a good example.

Almighty and everlasting God, who did enkindle the flame of your love in the heart of your servant Monnica: Grant to us, your humble servants, the same faith and power of love; that, as we rejoice in her triumph, we may profit by her example; through Jesus Christ our Lord.

Dame Julian of Norwich

Nun

Writer and Teacher

Dame Julian, or Lady Julian, so named from her gentle birth, was born in 1342. She claimed to be a simple, unlettered person; but though she was not learned, she was by no means uneducated. She knew her Bible and the teachings of the church, and she could express herself in vigorous English. It is possible, though there is no proof, that she became a Benedictine nun. On May 8, 1373, at the age of thirty, she received a series of "Sixteen Shewings" which are recorded in the first version of her *Revelations of Divine Love.* These came in response to prayers for "three gifts from God": to have the mind of Christ's Passion, a bodily sickness, and the gift of three wounds—contrition, compassion, and a "willful longing toward God." Some twenty years later her *Revelations* were expanded as a result of "inward teaching."

After the experience of 1373 she retired, with a personal servant, to a hermitage in the churchyard of St. Julian, Conisford, Norwich, so situated that she could witness the celebration of Mass in the church and receive visitors. The date of her death is unknown. The latest document that mentions her is dated 1416. Her book reveals tender meditation on the Passion of Christ and the mystery of the Holy Trinity, combined with a keen intellect and shrewd common sense, and a concern for the salvation of Jews and pagans. Her remarkable sense of balance and proportion is exhibited in her *Revelations.*

Gregory of Nazianzus

Died May 9, 389

Bishop of Constantinople

A Great Model Pastor

Gregory was a bishop's son, well off financially, and educated at the very finest schools of his day, including the universities of Alexandria and Athens. Among his school comrades was Basil (see June 14), and when he finished school Gregory participated in Basil's pioneer monastic community on the island of Pontus. However, he had no intention at that time of entering the priesthood. Then his father called him home and virtually thrust holy orders upon him. Gregory took the priestly office very seriously and was terrified at having it foisted upon him. He fled back to Pontus and, by much prayer, fasting, and soul searching, became reconciled to this new vocation.

The ecclesiastical career thus launched was to become a most distinguished one. Gregory was soon elected Bishop of Sasina. He was one of the most effective preachers against the Arian heresy.

The imperial city, Constantinople, was in the hands of the Arians and was ruled by the Arian emperor, Valens. When the emperor died in battle and the city was reopened to orthodox Christians, Gregory was the first bishop to enter the city. He was chiefly responsible for the reconversion of the city and he eventually became its bishop. He skillfully led his people through a time of violence and discord in the church, avoiding controversy over all but the most essential issues. "It is unwise for those who walk the high tight rope to lean to either side."

Florence Nightingale

Nurse

The Lady of the Lamp

The suffering wounded soldiers of the Crimean War name her "The Lady of the Lamp." When the fighting ended at sunset and the corpses of the dead and the bodies of the wounded lay strewn about, "Sister" Florence Nightingale, with her lamp, would appear and help. To this day her name is a symbol of courage and compassion.

She was born of British parents in Florence, Italy, was a devoted Anglican and, in fact, sought holy orders at a time when the church was not well disposed to grant such to females. She studied nursing with the Roman Catholic Sisters of Charity in Alexandria, Egypt, and with the Lutheran deaconesses at Kaiserswerth in Germany. Her attention was drawn to the hideous lack of care for the wounded of the British army and her valiant efforts single-handedly to reform the situation brought her both fame and infamy, for some considered her no more than a camp follower.

She returned to England after the Crimean War and founded the Nightingale School of Nursing at St. Thomas' Hospital, London, but her health had been broken by months of overexertion in the war and she was a near invalid. She wrote *Notes on Nursing* which became a standard text for nurses throughout the English-speaking world.

Dunstan

Died May 19, 988

Archbishop of Canterbury

Reformer of State and Church

By the tenth century England was exhausted through invasion and tribal warfare. Monastic life had degenerated, with few monks and fewer still who took seriously their vows and rules. Then a young monk appeared on the scene at Glastonbury monastery. His name was Dunstan and he was inspired to rejuvenate the lagging monasteries and revive the weary country. At Glastonbury he was instrumental in instituting the rigorous Benedictine Rule, and he got the scriptorium, a center for serious study, reopened. Finally, he was elected Abbot.

As the good reputation of Glastonbury spread, the new Abbot was inevitably drawn into politics. He served as Royal Treasurer to King Edred and under King Edgar he became, successively, Bishop of Worcester, of London, and finally Archbishop of Canterbury.

As Archbishop, Dunstan put all his resources to work to strengthen and rebuild the decaying and war-ravaged church in England. Among a people who knew almost nothing save the art of warfare, he preached and taught the skills of peace, industry, and learning. Schools, monasteries, farms, and shops reappeared on the English countryside. Slavery, debauchery, and concubinage waned. The authority of the church was respected and England enjoyed a peace and unity unknown before.

O God, we thank you for the ministry of Dunstan.

Alcuin

Died May 20, 804

Deacon, and Abbot of Tours

Inspirer of the Carolingian Renaissance

A breath of fresh air swept across Western Europe in what we call the "Age of Charlemagne." There was relative peace, security, and prosperity. Learning and the arts revived. The leading spirit of this renaissance was Alcuin of York.

Alcuin was the foremost teacher of his day. He revived "letters." Indeed, he is credited with the invention of the running script we use today. He was a competent theologian, poet, and author. He was a pioneer in conceiving the "idea of a university."

After serving for some years as Master of the Cathedral School in York, England, he traveled to Italy to study. There he met Charlemagne and they became fast friends. Alcuin served as royal tutor and as the great king's chief advisor in religious and educational matters. In 796 he became Abbot of the monastery at Tours, France, and there he founded a famous library and school. From there he exercised great influence in correcting misunderstandings of the Christian Faith and in discouraging practices which seemed inconsistent with this Faith, both in morals and in forms of worship.

We beseech you to shed upon your whole Church the bright beams of your light and peace, and help us to follow the good example of your servant Alcuin.

57

Jackson Kemper

Bishop

Missionary to the American Mid-West

The first Missionary Bishop of the Episcopal Church was also one of the greatest. A well-bred New Yorker and a pupil of Bishop Hobart (see September 12), his missionary activity began close to home, in Pennsylvania. He convinced the elderly Bishop White of Pennsylvania to visit the western portion of his diocese and then accompanied him on this journey.

The General Convention in 1835 consecrated him and sent him to the wilds of Indiana and Missouri. He found that there was but one church in each of these states. However, by 1850, thanks largely to the efforts of Jackson Kemper, both were flourishing dioceses with bishops of their own. Bishop Kemper toured the deep South, but the church was already prospering there. For "breathing space and room for expansion" he moved on into the Old Northwest. Wisconsin became his headquarters for the remainder of his life. He founded Nashotah House and from there he directed and conducted missionary activities in Iowa, Illinois, and Minnesota.

Here was a man of great vision and inexhaustible energy. More than any other single man, he built the Province of the Midwest.

Raise up, we pray you, in every land, heralds and evangelists of your kingdom, like your servant Jackson.

The Venerable Bede

Died May 25, 735

Priest, and Monk of Jarrow

Historian and Scholar

When the monks of Jarrow sang, "Lord, leave us not as orphans," it is said that Bede would often weep. As a child he was left orphaned in a dark, hostile, and dangerous land. He was cared for and reared by kindly monks. When he was but a youngster, plague struck the monastery, decimating it. The only surviving souls were Bede and the old Abbot. Bede naturally had a strong sense of the importance of community, of the fine line between life and death, and of our utter dependence upon the Creator.

He rarely ventured outside the walls of Jarrow monastery, yet his knowledge of theology, geography, and language was worthy of the most sophisticated of his time in Western Europe. He wrote a number of excellent books on various subjects, but he is best remembered for his *Ecclesiastical History of the English People.* This work has justly earned for him the title, "Father of English History." Unlike some of the careless historians of his day, he was meticulous in listing his authorities and sources. He takes care to separate known fact from hearsay, but his descriptions are lively and dramatic.

Bede thought of himself as a teacher, and he seems to have built most of his teaching around the Divine Offices which the monks read daily. It is altogether fitting that he was pronounced a "Doctor of the Church" by Pope Leo XIII. Bede's remains rest in Durham.

Augustine

First Archbishop of Canterbury

Apostle to the Anglo-Saxons

Augustine and a group of monks were sent to Britain by Pope Gregory (see March 12) in 597. Three centuries prior to this Christianity had been introduced to the British Isles, during the Roman occupation (see June 22 and March 1 and 17). However, when the Roman forces withdrew, the pagan Anglo-Saxons invaded the Isles and forced the Christians to flee into the hills and forests of Wales, Scotland, and Ireland, or to face a tenuous existence in England. Augustine found that his task was not only to convert the Anglo-Saxons but also to reestablish contacts between the British (or "Celtic") and Roman Churches.

Now Augustine seems to have been a rather timid and reticent fellow who had accepted this assignment with something less than enthusiasm. He did not speak the Anglo-Saxon tongue and was terrified at the prospect of confronting these notorious savages. He was relieved and delighted upon landing in Britain to find that the Anglo-Saxon queen, Bertha, was already a Christian and that the king was not unfriendly. The latter, King Ethelbert, eventually was converted and in time most of his subjects followed suit. Augustine established his cathedral at Canterbury in Kent. This was destined to become the most important bishophric in England and the mother diocese of the Anglican Communion. Archbishops of Canterbury are still said to hold the "Chair of Augustine."

The Visitation of the Blessed Virgin Mary

Mary Visits Elizabeth, Mother of John the Baptist

According to Luke's Gospel, Mary, immediately after being told of the forthcoming birth of Jesus, went to visit her cousin, Elizabeth. Elizabeth was also pregnant and her child was to be John the Baptist. This famous visit was important for several reasons.

When Elizabeth saw Mary, the baby leaped in her womb, not an uncommon experience in pregnancy but in this case regarded as a supernatural occurrence, signifying little John's excitement at the presence of the Saviour whom he was to proclaim. Elizabeth was the first to recognize Mary as the Mother of the Lord, exclaiming "Blessed art thou among women and blessed is the fruit of thy womb!"

The moving and eloquent canticle, *Magnificat,* is recorded by Luke at this point. It is called the "Song of Mary" and although it could hardly have been a stenographers report of what the blessed Mother said at the time, it most surely reflects her sentiments and the kind of response she must have expressed.

Father in heaven, who chose in wondrous grace the blessed Virgin Mary to be the mother of your incarnate Son: Grant that, as we honor the exaltation of her lowliness, so we may follow the example of her humble obedience to your will; through Jesus Christ your Son our Lord, who now lives and reigns with you and the Holy Spirit, one God, in glory everlasting.

Justin

Martyr at Rome

Early Christian Apologist

An apologist is one who attempts to make clear the grounds for his belief or course of action, one who attempts to explain to others the truth and validity of what he stands for. Justin was such an apologist for the early church.

He was born in Samaria but was a gentile and a pagan. As a young man he engaged in a long struggle for truth and meaning. He was for a time a Stoic, later a Pythagorean, and then a Platonist. Finally, in the ancient "melting pot" of Ephesus, he embraced Christianity, which he continued to regard as the most sublime revelation of truth to his very death.

Eventually Justin went to Rome and there, for some fifteen years, he operated a Christian school. He was not exceptionally skilled in either philosophy or literature, nor was he very original, but he compiled in his *Apologies* the most convincing and most popular arguments for Christianity extant. His strong, clear Christian witness became more than the Roman authorities could bear. He was prosecuted for atheism and found guilty. He and a group of his disciples were scourged and beheaded.

Almighty God, who did give your servant Justin boldness to confess the Name of our Saviour Jesus Christ before the rulers of this world: Grant that we likewise may ever be ready to give a reason for the hope that is in us.

The Martyrs of Lyons

First Martyrs in France

Lyons in Gaul (France) was the scene of one of the most terrible persecutions the early church had to endure. The Christians there were accused, as elsewhere, of atheism, blasphemy, treason, sexual perversion, and cannibalism. The Governor, hoping to please the Emperor Marcus Aurelius, staged public trials which lasted for several days and in which the populace was stirred into a mad frenzy against the Christians. Many were imprisoned, tortured, and beaten to death. Their remains were thrown to the dogs.

Among those mentioned by name in Eusebius' moving account was Alexander, a physician who was publicly roasted. He professed Christ and, when asked what God's name was, he replied, "God has no name as men have." As he expired he pointed out to the pagans that they were the ones who consumed human flesh. There was Blandina, "a blessed woman" who, "like a noble athlete," endured days of excruciating torture, abuse, and humiliation, saying only, "I am a Christian woman and nothing wicked happens among us." She was gored to death by a bull in the arena. Then there was the notable citizen Attalus, the elderly Bishop Pothinus, a deacon from Vienna, Sanctus, and a lad of fifteen, Ponticus. These and many others were subjected to brutal horrors and torments and were finally killed. Undaunted, they passed out of this world joyfully and victoriously, witnesses to the only living Lord.

The Martyrs of Uganda

Martyrs of Modern Africa

Africa boasts the world's oldest Christian kingdom extant, Ethiopia, and also some of the newest Christian countries. Uganda in East Africa is one. A former British protectorate, it is now an independent republic and a part of the British Commonwealth.

Christianity was introduced to Uganda by Anglican and Roman Catholic missionaries in the nineteenth century. They were well received by the powerful King of Buganda, Mutesa. However, he was not converted, and he was succeeded by King Mwanga, a degenerate and perverse individual who sought a return to primitive animism. He expelled missionaries and began systematically terrorizing the native Christians. Many were flogged and mutilated. In 1884 three youths were burned to death for their faith. They were said to have approached martyrdom singing the favorite Swahili hymn, "Daily, daily sing the praises." We do not know how many Christians died in this persecution but, between May 25th and June 3rd, 1886, at least thirty-two were martyred, most of them on a great pyre at Namugongo.

Out of these afflictions, however, grew a strong indigenous church, a symbol of resurgent Christianity in Africa and of successful cooperation between Anglicans and Roman Catholics.

Grant us so to cherish the blessed Martyrs of Uganda that we may share their steadfast faith.

Boniface

Archbishop of Mainz

Missionary to Germany, and Martyr

One of the great achievements of the Anglo-Saxon Christians was the conversion of their cousins in Germany. The trail was blazed by Willibrord (see November 7) but the man to whom most credit is due was Boniface of Devonshire, England. His real name was Wynfrith. Boniface ("good deeds") was a nickname that stuck.

In spite of some disappointing efforts in Frisia (Holland), the missionary, Boniface, proceeded into the Germanic heartland. In Bavaria, Thuringia, and Hesse he won many converts to Christ. In an act of extraordinary boldness, he chopped down the sacred Oak of Thor at Geismar. With the felling of this tree, Germanic confidence in the old gods fell. From then on Boniface's work progressed rapidly. He soon organized eight German dioceses, founded the famous Abbey at Fulda, and was himself consecrated the first Archbishop of Mainz. Boniface always kept in close touch with England, writing many letters to friends at home who supplied him with books, vestments, and recruits for the work in Germany.

Still concerned about the Frisians with whom he had failed, Boniface made another effort to revive the church there. In this attempt he was slain by a mob of Frisian pagans near Utrecht.

Thank you for your servant Boniface.

Columba

Abbot of Iona

Apostle of Scotland

In the troubled and violent Dark Ages in Northern Europe monasteries served as inns, orphanages, centers of learning, and even as fortresses. The light of civilization flickered dimly and might have gone out altogether had it not been for these convent-shelters.

Columba, a stern and strong monk from Ireland, founded three such establishments. He founded the monasteries of Derry and Durrow on his native island, and Iona on the coast of Scotland. Iona was the center of operations for the conversion of the Scots and Picts and became the most famous religious house in Scotland. There Columba baptised Brude, King of the Picts, and later a King of the Scots came to this Abbot of the "Holy Isle" for baptism.

The historian Bede tells us that Columba led many to Christianity by his "preaching and example." He was much admired for his physical as well as spiritual prowess. He was a vigorous ascetic and was still quite active when he died, nearly eighty years old. The memory of Columba lives on in Scotland, and Iona, though desecrated during the Reformation, is today a Protestant religious community.

Almighty God, you did choose your servant Columba to be an apostle to the people of Scotland, to bring those who were wandering in darkness to your true light: Grant us to walk in that same light.

Ephrem of Edessa

Deacon

Syrian Doctor of the Church

Christianity flourished early in Syria, and Antioch was a major center of the church. Although that land is today dominated by Moslems, the Syrian Orthodox Church still has well over a million members in the world. One of the great fathers of the church in Syria was Ephrem of Edessa.

Ephrem was the head of a very successful Christian school in Edessa, Syria. There he championed the Nicene faith, and in fact he may have been present in Nicaea for the famous council which met there in 325. He became well known for the austerity and sanctity of his life as well as for his learning. His writings are voluminous and include biblical commentaries, essays on dogma, history, and biography, as well as a host of hymns. Many of the latter have long been an integral part of Syrian Orthodox worship.

The Anglican Communion has long enjoyed warm and friendly relations with the Syrian Church. Ephrem's feast would seem an appropriate time to give thanks to God for this relationship and for the witness of the Syrian Christians today and through the ages.

Almighty God, who enriched your Church with the singular learning and holiness of your Deacon Ephrem: Grant us to hold fast the true doctrine of your Son our Saviour Jesus Christ, and to fashion our lives according to the same, to the glory of your great Name.

Basil the Great

Died June 14, 379

Bishop of Caesarea

An Eastern Father of the Church

More than any other single man, Basil, Bishop of Caesarea in Cappadocia (modern central Turkey), was responsible for the shaping of the Eastern Church. He was handsome, brilliant, wealthy, and educated in the finest schools of his day. He did not turn from poverty of body or intellect to Christianity. He was a close friend of Gregory Nazianzus (see May 9) and his brother was Gregory of Nyssa (see March 9). He was an eloquent preacher and a most persuasive statesman. He was one of the key figures in the triumph of Christian orthodoxy over Arianism. He was a major contributor to the Divine Liturgy of the Eastern Church which bears his name. Early in his career he founded a monastery on the island of Pontus, and he put forward the monastic rule that still prevails in the Eastern Church.

Basil would accept no interpretation of the gospel that called for anything less than radical social action. He founded hospitals and organized a massive program for the relief of the poor, both of which were successful then and for many generations after his death. He called the rich Christians of his city "thieves," saying, "What other name does he deserve who, being able to clothe the naked, yet refuses? . . . The clothes you store away belong to the naked; the shoes that molder in your closet belong to those who have none. . . ."

Grant us to hold fast to Basil's faith.

Evelyn Underhill

June 15, 1941

Theologian and Mystic

Tutor of Christian Mysticism

In the first half of the 20th century a spiritual reawakening began to stir among English-speaking Christians, especially among Anglicans. The pioneer lay leader of this movement was an English woman, Evelyn Underhill. The offspring of this movement, such as Charles Williams, T.S. Eliot, Dorothy Sayers and C.S. Lewis, would owe her a debt of gratitude, particularly for her classic work, *Mysticism,* first published in 1911. However, she not only wrote about the great Christian mystic tradition, she practiced it and became one of the foremost spiritual directors of her time. Probably her most famous book, simply entitled *Worship,* was written after many years' experience as a retreat leader.

Evelyn Underhill successfully reminded us that *adoration* is the soul of prayer, both common and private, and helped liberate Anglicans from the sterile rationalism, pedagogy or exhortation that often went under the name of "worship." She revived the church's appreciation of the way of the mystics, reminding us that the true Christian mystic's life is not "withdrawn from common duties into some rapturous dreamland ... The hard and devoted life of the great mystics of the Church at once contradicts this view. It is a life inspired by a vivid and definite aim; the life of a dedicated will moving steadily in one direction, towards a perfect and unbroken union with God."

Joseph Butler

Died June 16, 1752

Bishop of Durham

Scholar and Pastor

The English Church in the eighteenth century was besieged by Deists, Non-Conforming Evangelicals, and most of all by indifferent or lazy clergy of her own. Joseph Butler was an outstanding example of the "other side of the coin." Operating well within the structures and traditions of the Established Church, he forged a positive Christian apologetic which has outlived the attitudes of his opponents. He is credited with breaking the force of Deism in England, without compromising his reason, and with saving many from fanatic Evangelicalism, without surrendering his warmth, personal piety, or social concern. His masterpiece, the *Analogy of Religion,* is still considered one of the most reasoned and convincing defenses of Christian faith and ethic.

Butler first established a reputation as a preacher at the Rolls Chapel, London, where his famous *Fifteen Sermons* were delivered and published. He wrote the *Analogy of Religion* under very different circumstances, as rector of the small parish of Stanhope in the North of England. He was elected Bishop of Bristol and served most admirably in that post for twelve years before accepting the bishophric of Durham in which position he died. Bishop Butler was a great pastor, who served the minds as well as the bodies and spirits of his people.

We thank you for the teaching of your servant Joseph; may our witness be as faithful.

Bernard Mizeki

Martyr in Rhodesia

As a teenager Bernard Mizeki fled from the oppression of his native Portuguese East Africa, escaping to Capetown, South Africa. There he was educated, converted, and baptised by Anglican missionaries.

At age thirty he volunteered to serve as a teacher at a small pioneer mission in Mashonaland, Southern Rhodesia. There, in isolated and primitive Nhowa, he worked for five years, gaining many converts and breaking the spell that superstition and ignorance had for so long held over the people.

These were very troubled times in Rhodesia and missionaries were often regarded as the "stooges" of European imperialists. So it was with Bernard Mizeki. When a native uprising occurred in 1896 he was warned to flee, but, not regarding himself as an enemy of the natives, and not wishing to leave his recent converts, he remained. He was brutally stabbed to death. Afterwards his body, mysteriously, was never found. Today, a shrine at the sight of his martyrdom attracts many pilgrims.

Almighty God, by whose grace and power your holy martyr Bernard triumphed over suffering, and was faithful even to death: Grant us, who now remember him in thanksgiving, to be so faithful in our witness to you in this world, that we may receive with him the crown of everlasting life; through Jesus Christ our Lord, who lives and reigns with you and the Holy Spirit forever.

Alban

First Martyr of Britain

"In Britain's Isle was holy Alban born." Alban was a young pagan who lived in the Roman town of Verulamium (modern St. Albans, Hertfordshire, just north of London). During the persecution of Diocletian (some historians think Decius), he sheltered a Christian priest in his home. The priest converted and baptised him. Later, when Roman soldiers came to search the house, Alban hid the priest and disguised himself in the priest's cloak. He was dragged off to court. When it was discovered who he was and what he had done he was accused of harboring a rebelious and sacrilegious person. Alban then publicly confessed his faith in Jesus Christ, was scourged and, still persisting in his confession, was sentenced to death. The executioner refused to do his duty and he and the priest, whose names we do not know, soon became the second and third British martyrs.

Alban has always been highly honored among British Christians. St. Alban's Abbey was a great medieval monument to him and there his shrine still stands.

Almighty God, by whose grace and power your holy martyr Alban triumphed over suffering, and despised death: Grant, we beseech you, that enduring hardness, and waxing valiant in fight, we may with the noble army of martyrs receive the crown of everlasting life; through Jesus Christ our Lord.

Irenaeus

Bishop of Lyons

A Western Father of the Church

Scarcely had the blood of the Martyrs of Lyons (see June 2) dried before Irenaeus was consecrated Bishop of Lyons. He had narrowly escaped the persecution himself, being on church business in Rome at the time.

As a lad Irenaeus had learned the Christian faith at the knee of Polycarp (see February 23) in his native Smyrna. After a period of study in Rome he moved to Gaul (France) where he was elected bishop. He served Lyons in that capacity for a quarter of a century and during that time sufficiently influenced the whole church that he came to be regarded as one of the Fathers.

Irenaeus wrote a number of significant letters, an essay entitled "The Demonstration of Apostolic Preaching," and a major work *Against Heresies,* all in Greek. He was an avid student of the Holy Scriptures, a tireless pastor, and the first great theologian of the Western Church. He was a champion of orthodoxy against Gnosticism, a champion of episcopal polity and of the canonical Scriptures. Today's heirs of Irenaeus live the life of faith expounded in the church's doctrine, are loyal to their bishops and pastors, and diligently study the Holy Bible.

Almighty God, who did uphold your servant Irenaeus with strength to maintain the truth against every wind of vain doctrine: We beseech you to keep us steadfast in your true religion, and to walk in constancy.

Peter and Paul

Apostles and Martyrs

Peter and Paul are commemorated individually on January 18th and January 25th, respectively. However, following an ancient custom, we remember them together on this the presumed date of their martyrdom. Christian tradition has long held that these two stalwart leaders of the early church died together in the Neronian persecution of 64 A.D.

In so many ways Peter and Paul were very different from one another. Paul was a well educated and cosmopolitan Jew of the Diaspora, reared in the sophisticated city of Tarsus. Peter was an uneducated provincial and a fisherman. Peter was the more conservative of the two, as one might expect, and it is not surprising that they had strong differences of opinion. They were leaders of opposing points of view at the first church council in Jerusalem. However, their common commitment to Christ and his church proved far stronger than their individual points of view. In the risen Lord they found reconciliation and, fittingly, they died together, crucified as he had been.

Nero thought he had found "the final solution to the Christian problem." On the contrary, the church was "nourished by the blood of her martyrs" and it was Christ, the Lord of Peter and Paul, who was ultimately to triumph, not Nero.

Grant that your household the Church may be instructed by their teaching and example.

Benedict of Nursia

Abbot of Monte Cassino

Founder of Western Monasticism

The serious breakdown of society and authority in 5th century Europe led to the downfall of many men and caused many others simply to run away from society and hide as hermits, hating and despairing of mankind. Benedict of Nursia rejected both of these alternatives. Instead he entered on a brave new venture. At Subiaco, and later at Monte Cassino (both in Italy), he founded the first monastic communities of Western Europe.

He drafted a firm but reasonable "Rule" (i.e. constitution) for these communities. He was never ordained and his communities were composed only of laymen at first. Their lives centered around the daily offices. When they were not praying and studying scripture, they were engaged in manual labor and in works of charity. Like the early Christians, they held all property in common.

Benedict attracted little attention in his own lifetime, but after his death, as the monasteries grew and spread so did his fame. The "Benedictine" monasteries became little islands where a man could still learn to love God and his fellow man and truly practice the Christian religion in his whole life. These communities operated schools, orphanages, hospitals, and assumed many of the functions of state.

Benedictine monks were largely responsible for the conversion and civilization of England. Westminster Abbey was for centuries a Benedictine house. Nashdom Abbey is its modern center in England.

William White

Bishop of Pennsylvania

First Presiding Bishop of the American Church

At the conclusion of the American Revolution there was grave concern among churchmen, many of whom had stoutly supported the Revolution, that the Anglican Church might succumb as a disastrous side-effect of that Revolution.

One of the most tireless and effective workers for an autonomous Episcopal Church in the U.S.A. was the Rev. William White, Rector of Christ Church, Philadelphia, and former Chaplain of the Continental Congress. Appropriately, he became the first American bishop consecrated in the English line. He was a quiet and scholarly man and an intimate friend of some of the prominent leaders of both America and England. As a clergyman in Philadelphia he had exhibited an unusual sensitivity for the poor, the unfortunate, and those who were in trouble. He was president of the Philadelphia Dispensary, which supplied medical aid to the poor; of the Pennsylvania Institute for the Deaf and Dumb; and of the Philadelphia Society for Alleviating the Miseries of Public Prisons. He was concerned about religious education, was instrumental in the founding of the first Episcopal Sunday School in America.

On February 4th, 1787, in Lambeth Chapel, London, William White was consecrated by the Archbishop of Canterbury, John Moore, and two other bishops. He returned immediately to America and became the first Presiding Bishop of the Episcopal Church in the U.S.A.

Mary Magdalene

A Disciple of the Lord

Mary of Magdala (Magdalene) was one of several women of ill repute whose lives were radically changed by Jesus. She was said to be "possessed by seven demons" and was considered "lost," beyond redemption, by the authorities of that time. The scriptures are not explicit about the nature of her many sins, but it is made very clear that Jesus gave her the will and power to abandon them. Nevertheless, the authorities were not impressed and Jesus seems to have been criticized for keeping the company of such people.

Tradition has held that she was a very emotional person and our English word "maudlin" derives from her name. Mary of Magdala followed Jesus into Galilee and helped care for him and the disciples there. She witnessed the Lord's suffering on the cross. She took oil to anoint his entombed body and therefore she is often represented with a jar of ointment. Her tearful reaction finding an empty tomb is still a favorite line to many faithful, "They have taken my Lord away and I do not know where they have laid him." When the Lord appeared and called her name, "Mary," she recognized him and exclaimed, "My Master!" She was the first to see the risen Lord.

Mercifully grant that by your grace we may be healed of all our infirmities and, like your servant Mary, be restored to health of body and of mind.

Thomas a Kempis

Died July 24, 1471

Priest

Scholar, Pastor, and Author

Few if any books, save the Holy Scriptures, have had as profound an effect on Christian piety as *The Imitation of Christ* by Thomas a Kempis. The author eloquently advances the notion that, "Whosoever would fully and feelingly understand the words of Christ, must endeavor to conform his life wholly to the life of Christ." The theme of the book is set forth in its first sentence, a quotation from the Gospel of John. " 'He that followeth me walketh not in darkness,' saith the Lord." The last part of the book contains a form of self-examination for use before receiving Holy Communion. Many Christians, both Catholic and Protestant, still find this a most helpful guide in their devotional lives.

Thomas led a relatively quiet and unspectacular life as a priest at the Augustinian convent of Mount St. Agnes, near Zwolle, in the Netherlands. He was born and named Thomas Hammerken at Kempen, a small town near Dusseldorf in Germany. He was educated by the Brothers of the Common Life, one of the most famous teaching orders of that time. He pursued a scholarly and contemplative life, but became famous as a preacher, and his advice and counsel was often sought by men and women of all walks of life.

Grant that we may follow the good example of your servant Thomas, and hold fast the faith.

Anne and Joachim

The Parents of the Blessed Virgin Mary

We have little historical information concerning the parents of Mary, although we have a wealth of legend and tradition. Anne has long been honored in the naming of countless churches, hospitals, guilds, and various charitable institutions. Her feast is universally celebrated and she is the patroness of Brittany.

Joachim, husband of Anne and father of Mary, has received less attention. We know nothing about him, save his name, and even that is controversial.

Perhaps this date is an appropriate time to reflect on the importance of parenthood. What kind of influence are we having on our children? Do our lives reflect the best in the care and training we received from our parents? All we really know about Anne and Joachim is an inference from the kind of daughter they reared.

O almighty God, who has called us to faith in you, and has compassed us about with so great a cloud of witnesses: Grant that we, encouraged by the good examples of your Saints, and especially of your servants Anne and Joachim, may persevere in running the race that is set before us, until at length, through your mercy, we with them attain to your eternal joy; through him who is the author and finisher of our faith, your Son Jesus Christ our Lord.

William Reed Huntington

Priest

19th Century Church Leader

If any one man could be seen as typifying the spirit of the Episcopal Church in the 19th century, it would probably be W. R. Huntington, a priest from Massachusetts who was Rector of Grace Church, New York City, for over twenty-five years. Dr. Huntington was a leader in the House of Deputies for thirteen consecutive General Conventions (1871-1907). He was one of the designers of the Prayer Book revision of 1892 and he led the movement to revive the order of deaconesses in the Episcopal Church.

He profoundly influenced the course of ecumenical relations with his book, *The Church Idea—An Essay Toward Unity,* which first advanced the concept of a reunion of the universal church on the basis of mutual acceptance of the scriptures, the creeds, the sacraments, and the historic episcopate. This became the famous "Lambeth Quadrilateral" and the foundation on which Anglican discussions of unity with other Christian bodies have taken place the world over.

Dr. Huntington, living in the time of the "Monkey Trial" and other crises which pitted religion and science against one another, said, "the theologians and naturalists are allies. Truth is truth, however and whencesoever obtained, and we can never have occasion to be either afraid of it or unthankful for it."

Inspire us, Lord, as you did your servant William.

Mary and Martha of Bethany

Companions of the Lord

Mary and Martha lived with their brother, Lazarus, at Bethany, a village not far from Jerusalem. They seem to have been very sensitive and compassionate girls and gladly entertained Jesus and the disciples in their home. Mary; on one occasion, anointed Jesus' feet with expensive oil in an outpouring of emotion and love which drew criticism from some of the disciples. To them this act seemed sentimental and wasteful. On another occasion Mary was criticised by Martha for neglecting her household duties in order to "sit at the feet of Jesus." On both of these occasions Jesus came to the defense of Mary.

It was Martha who met Jesus when he came to her family on the death of Lazarus and who confidently testified that had he been there Lazarus would not have died. It was to Martha that Jesus said, "I am the resurrection and the life. . . ."

Jesus had no more loyal and generous followers than Mary and Martha of Bethany. Their examples of devotion and fidelity have inspired Christian women for generations.

Almighty and everlasting God, who enkindled the flame of your love in the heart of your servants Mary and Martha: Grant to us, your humble servants, a like faith and power of love; that, as we rejoice in their triumph, we may profit by their examples; through Jesus Christ our Lord.

William Wilberforce

Member of Parliament

Christian Statesman

So often a devout and well-informed layman is a far more effective servant of the church than a professional clergyman. William Wilberforce of Hull, England, is an excellent example. He was a devoted student of the New Testament and a strong churchman. He was educated at Cambridge University and traveled widely. A deep concern for the Lord and his work led Wilberforce to the "brink of Holy Orders." However, under the influence of John Newton, he decided that he could better serve Christ as a politician.

For over fifty years, William Wilberforce served the church, his country, and the world as a Member of Parliament and an eloquent spokesman for Christian values and ethics. He is probably best remembered for his efforts to end slavery in the British Empire. The crowning achievement of his legislative career, the Emancipation Act of 1833, was passed one month after his death. He also championed the cause of Catholic Emancipation in the British Isles, of English missions in India, of parliamentary reform, and of judicial and prison reform. He wrote *A Practical View of the Prevailing Religious System of Professed Christians,* which was widely read both in England and on the continent, and which significantly influenced religious and political thinking in his day.

May we also, like William, defend the poor.

Joseph of Arimathaea

The Gentleman in Whose Tomb Jesus was Buried

Joseph was a wealthy and pious Jew and a member of the Sanhedrin, the Council which tried Jesus. The Gospel according to Luke indicates that Joseph did not consent to the decision that Jesus be crucified, and other scriptures suggest that he may have absented himself from the trial. It is believed that he was a "secret" disciple of Christ, like Nicodemus.

After the crucifixion, Joseph displayed considerable courage in going to Pilate and asking for the privilege of burying the body of Jesus with proper care and ceremony. In fact, Joseph reverently laid the body of Jesus in the fine tomb he had prepared for himself. John's Gospel indicates that Nicodemus helped Joseph prepare the body for burial. Looking back today, being aware of the resurrection, we tend not to see just how loyal, generous, and, indeed, pathetic this gesture must have been.

There is a charming medieval legend that Joseph of Arimathaea came to England and founded Glastonbury Abbey of Arthurian fame. This may, in part, account for his continued popularity among English Christians.

O merciful God, by whose servant Joseph the body of our Lord and Saviour was committed to the grave with reverence and godly fear: Grant, we beseech you, to your faithful people grace and courage to serve and love Jesus with unfeigned devotion all the days of their life; through the same Jesus Christ our Lord.

Oswald

King and Martyr

Royal Evangelist of Northumbria

The conversion of the north of England in the 7th century began in a mysterious way with the decision of the heathen king of Northumbria, Aefelfrith the Destroyer, to send his children to the Island of Iona for safekeeping. There, the royal children, including Oswald, who was to become the next king of Northumbria, were cared for by Celtic Christian monks. There young Oswald met Aidan (see August 31). There he was baptized and tutored in the Christian faith.

When Oswald succeeded to the throne of Northumbria he and Aidan and their companions in Christ began the process of converting the people of this Anglo-Saxon kingdom to Christianity. Oswald earned a reputation for piety, compassion and learning. He was particularly renowned for his generosity and his efforts to relieve the poor and suffering.

On this day in 642 he was struck down by pagan Mercian soldiers and fell dead beneath the banner of the cross, which he had chosen as his ensign. The kingdom of Northumbria was eventually incorporated into the kingdom of England. The faith Oswald and the Celtic monks had planted remains in the north country of England.

John Mason Neale

Priest

Scholar of the Catholic Revival in the Church of England

The 19th century witnessed a reawakening of the Catholic spirit of the Church of England and in America. John Mason Neale was one of the prominent leaders in this revival. He was an eminent scholar of history and language, educated at Cambridge University and for twenty years the Warden of Sacksville College, East Grinsted.

He was a patient, modest, and devoted priest. He founded the Sisterhood of St. Margaret, a teaching and nursing order for women, and he weathered the storm of protests which arose over the establishment of it.

Neale was one of the most important hymn writers of the 19th century. *The Hymnal 1940* contains thirty-nine hymns either written or translated by him. Among these are such popular ones as, "Good Christian men rejoice," "All glory, laud, and honor," "Come ye faithful, raise the strain," and "Christ is made the sure foundation."

Always concerned about the education of children, Neale wrote numerous children's books. On the heavier side, some of his most impressive publications were *Commentary on the Psalms* (four volumes, 1864-1870) and *History of the Holy Eastern Church* (five volumes, 1847-1873). John Mason Neale awakened the minds of English and American Christians to the vast depth and breadth of their heritage.

Dominic

Died August 8, 1221

Priest and Friar

Orthodox Reformer in the Middle Ages

The church has often been tempted to deal harshly and angrily with heresy and sometimes to defeat her own purposes in so doing, betraying the Lord's own teaching. This seemed to be the case in the crusade against the Albigensian heretics. Dominic, a learned and pious Spanish aristocrat, became deeply concerned about the situation and founded an Order of Preachers whose special task was to combat heresy with sound learning and intelligent preaching, rather than with force of arms. Members of this order came to be called "Dominicans," or in England, "Blackfriars," because of their black habit.

The Dominicans produced some of the greatest scholars and teachers of medieval Europe, including Albertus Magnus and Thomas Aquinas. They contributed significantly to the rise of the universities.

Dominic was a prodigious organizer and designed for his order a form of representative government, unique among monastic orders of his day. Dominic's god-son, Simon de Montfort, became a powerful leader among the English barons, and the Angevin kings of England favored the Dominicans. Therefore, Dominic and his Order of Preachers, seems to have contributed to the development of English Parliamentary government.

Sadly, the Order eventually became guilty of the very sins it was founded to oppose, associating itself with the Spanish Inquisition and with the Conquistadores.

Laurence
Deacon

Roman Martyr

One of the ancient and sacred duties of a deacon is to distribute food and to care for the poor. Laurence was one deacon who certainly took that assignment seriously. He was the trusted "right hand man" of Bishop Sixtus II of Rome. When the Emperor, Valerian, had Bishop Sixtus jailed, the Bishop entrusted the whole treasury of the Church in Rome to Deacon Laurence. Laurence gave it all to the poor and sick. When Valerian learned that Laurence had been given the treasury of the church, he hauled the deacon into court and demanded that he turn over that treasury—the funds of an illegal organization. Laurence responded by assembling a mob of infirm and impoverished persons and presenting them to the ruler, saying, "These are the treasure of the Church!" Valerian was greatly angered by this and had Laurence publicly executed. Tradition says that he was roasted alive, slowly, on a skewer. We have no nobler testimony to the faith and character of the 3rd century Christian Church than that of Laurence, Deacon and Martyr.

Almighty God, by whose grace and power your holy Deacon and martyr Laurence triumphed over suffering, and despised death: Grant, we beseech you, that enduring hardiness, and waxing valiant in fight, we may with the noble army of martyrs receive the crown of everlasting life; through Jesus Christ our Lord.

Clare of Assisi

Founder of the Poor Clares

Clare, the daughter of a noble Italian family, was very deeply touched by the teaching of Francis of Assisi. She refused two proffered marriages and when eighteen years old joined a convent of Benedictine nuns. Later, her sister, and finally her widowed mother, joined her in this convent. Then, with the help of Francis himself, these three founded the first Franciscan community for women. It was located at St. Damian's Church in Assisi. The community grew and flourished. There the "Poor Ladies," or "Poor Clares" as they came to be called, observed the same strict rules of poverty, humility, and devotion that the male Franciscans observed.

Filled with evangelical fervor and compassion for the souls of her little flock, Clare became a model abbess. For forty years she wisely and firmly led the community and oversaw the founding of similar communities throughout Europe. No one ever better personified the Franciscan ideal of renunciation for Christ's sake.

There is today an Anglican community of Poor Clares at Oxford, England, and one on Long Island, New York.

O God of mercy, enlighten the hearts of your faithful people, and grant us after the example of your servant Clare, not to mind earthly things, but to love things heavenly; through Jesus Christ our Lord.

Jeremy Taylor

Bishop of Down, Connor, and Dromore

Anglican Stalwart in Troubled Times

When the times are very troubled, learning and moderation are rarely regarded as virtues. Jeremy Taylor was a superb scholar and a man of deep spiritual insight. His learning, piety, and good advice gained him little popularity or peace in 17th century Britain.

Taylor's writings, however, have stood the test of time. His *Holy Living and Holy Dying* is a masterpiece of devotional prose and a gem of Christian wisdom, characteristic of the finest in Anglican spirituality. It stresses balance and moderation and insists on the discipline and good order in religion.

Taylor was a graduate of Cambridge University, a professor at Oxford, and a close friend of many of the religious and political leaders of his day. He served for a time as a chaplain to King Charles I and when the Puritan revolution erupted he was loyal to his king and church. For this he was imprisoned and forced into seclusion for a time. It was then that he did much of his writing.

When the kingdom and church were restored in 1660, Taylor's loyalty was lavishly rewarded. He was made Bishop of Down and Connor and vice-chancellor of Dublin University. There he spent the last years of his life, trying to steer a straight course through Ireland's violent Roman Catholic and Presbyterian confrontations.

Mary, the Virgin

Mother of our Lord

The Mother of our Lord is certainly the most remembered and most important of the saints, considering her very special relationship to him. Early in Christian history, when some men denied that Jesus Christ was truly a man, Christians pointed to the fact that he was born of a woman and inserted the phrase "born of the Virgin Mary" into the creed to emphasize Jesus' humanity. Later, when some other men denied that Jesus was God the Son, Greek Christians began calling Mary "Theotokos," i.e. "Bearer of God," to emphasize Jesus' true Godship. One's understanding of Christ governs one's understanding of Mary and vice versa.

Mary is often seen as representative of the church, the special vehicle or bearer of God to mankind. She is seen as the ideal mother who patiently cared for her little son and quietly accepted the highly unusual circumstances of his birth, life, death, and resurrection. In the Daily Offices, the church continually remembers her in the canticle attributed to her by Luke, the "Magnificat." She is particularly honored on five special feasts in the Christian Year. Perhaps her cousin, Elizabeth, best summed up the feeling of the faithful towards Mary when she said, "Blessed is she who believed that there would be a fulfillment of what was spoken to her from the Lord."

* Purification, February, 2; Annunciation, March 25; Visitation, May 31; Nativity of our Lord, December 25.

William Porcher Dubose

Died August 18, 1918

Priest

American Theologian

A century ago in an obscure corner of Southern Appalachia there lived and died a man who has been acclaimed "the only important creative theologian that the Episcopal Church in the United States has produced." He lived a life which, had any one less than he lived it, would have been called tragic. Born and reared in a prominent South Carolina family, he graduated from the Citadel and from the University of Virginia and served with some distinction as a Confederate line officer. However, in the Civil War and its aftermath he lost his wealth, his health, his wife, and finally his little son. In the meantime he had received Holy Orders and accepted a call as chaplain to the small Episcopal University at Sewanee, Tennessee. There he founded a School of Theology which still survives and there he did his greatest work.

His writings, *The Soteriology of the New Testament, The Gospel in the Gospels, High Priesthood and Sacrifice,* and other books, although applauded in England, were ill-received in his native land. While Oxford dons were calling him "the wisest writer on both sides of the Atlantic," W. P. DuBose was being threatened with a heresy trial at home. He died without wealth or fame, but he had sung "the Lord's song in a strange land" and, as a later biographer was to observe, he was a "live voice in an age of many echoes."

Bernard

Abbot of Clairvaux

Christian Leader in the Middle Ages

Though his body was meager and emaciated from strict
monastic practices, the figure of Bernard of Clairvaux
towered over the 12th century church like a colossus.
This bold and forthright monk from Southern France,
the Abbot of Clairvaux, tutored by the devout and wise
Englishman, Stephen Harding, was the most eloquent
and effective leader of both church and state in his
generation. Bernard traveled widely, writing and speaking against the Albigensian heresy, against the Moslem
invasion of the Christian East, and against the Christian
mistreatment of Jews. He was drawn into every major
international conflict of his day, including disputed
Papal elections and the disastrous Second Crusade. But
his chief concern was for the renewal of the church.

Bernard supervised the founding of at least sixty new
monasteries. He taught absolute devotion to Christ and
to the mission of his body, the church. His popular
treatise *On the Love of God* still speaks clearly to those
who read it. He lamented the indolence and vain luxury
of many of the church's leaders, writing, "The church is
resplendent in her walls, beggarly in her poor. She
clothes her stones in gold, and leaves her sons naked!"

*Almighty and everlasting God, who did enkindle the
flame of your love in the heart of your servant Bernard:
Grant to us, your humble servants, the same faith and
power of love.*

Louis

King of France

Christian Monarch

In fiction and fancy King Louis IX of France is the "knight in shining armour" who gallantly led the French army in the Crusades. This idea of Louis is true, but this image emerged from a man of deep conviction and rigorous self-discipline.

Louis is best remembered in France as a peacemaker and law-giver. He curbed the private feudal warfare that had for years ravaged France and significantly reformed the taxing and judicial systems of the kingdom. He had a good sense of justice and fairness and tried to see that every man, peasant or prince, got his "day in court."

Strong in the Christian faith, he was a staunch opponent of the Albigensian heresy in France, but he was no bigot. He never made unreasonable demands on his enemies. Even the Arabs admired him, and his traditional enemies at home, the English, respected him so much that they asked him to arbitrate in their disputes among themselves.

Louis was a patron of learning and the arts. He was one of the founders of the University of Paris (the Sorbonne) and the grand cathedrals of Amiens, Bourges, and Chartres were largely built during his reign and with his patronage. Certainly the medieval ideal of Christian kingship was realized in the person of Louis IX.

Thomas Gallaudet
Priest
Henry Winter Syle
Priest

Apostles to the Deaf

Other churchmen had responded to the lonely cry of the deaf, but the Rev. Thomas Gallaudet of Hartford, Connecticut, first brought to national attention their plight. After studying the latest European methods in France and England, he opened his school for the deaf in Hartford in 1817. Within the next half century over a score of public schools for the deaf had been spawned by this school.

His son, also the Rev. Thomas Gallaudet, was able to concentrate more explicitly on the spiritual welfare of the deaf and to this end he dedicated his life. He was the rector of St. Stephen's Church in Philadelphia. Among his disciples was Henry Syle. Syle was born of Episcopal missionary parents in China and became deaf at age six. Yet, he was able to secure a substantial education at Trinity College, Hartford, and earned a master's degree from Yale University. Although totally deaf, he was able to serve as a lay reader at St. Stephen's Church in Philadelphia. There he read for orders and it was in that church that he became the first deaf person ever ordained in America, perhaps in the world. Henry Syle, who never fully recovered from health problems that resulted from the environment of his early years in China, was an indefatigable servant of Christ and of the deaf. In 1888 he founded All Souls' Church for the Deaf in Philadelphia.

Augustine

Bishop of Hippo

Church Father

Augustine (not to be confused with Augustine of Canterbury) would be very much at home with some of today's collegians. He was reared in a "half-Christian" home which he left in search of truth. He "co-habitated" with a girl whom he was always to love but never to formally marry. She bore him a son who was the "apple of his eye." Augustine seriously sought the counsel of astrologers and all kinds of spiritual advisors and philosophers. He was a sincere Manichaean and, later, a convinced Platonist. Finally, under the influence of Ambrose, the great old Bishop of Milan, Augustine turned to "the Man from Galilee."

With the possible exception of Paul of Tarsus, no one has affected the Christian tradition, way of life, and thought, as profoundly as Augustine.

His autobiography, *Confessions,* his treatise, *On the Trinity,* and his famous essays, *On the City of God,* remain classics of Christian literature second only to the scripture itself. Much of modern Catholic and Protestant theology and practice derives from his original work.

Augustine eventually entered the priesthood and later was consecrated Bishop of Hippo in North Africa. He witnessed the sack of the city of Rome by Alaric, and as he lay on his deathbed Vandals were assaulting his own city of Hippo.

Help us to follow Augustine's example.

Aidan

Bishop of Lindisfarne

Apostle of Northern England

It has often been observed that "actions speak louder than words" and that the best kind of Christian evangelism is that which proceeds from godly and charitable living. Aidan provides us with an example of just that.

Trained at Iona, Scotland's "Holy Isle," Aidan was already revered as a compassionate and well learned monk, when King Oswald of Northumbria invited him to come and help with the evangelization of Northern England. Aidan joyfully responded and began the work by founding a monastery on the Island of Lindisfarne. This monastery soon became a center for missionary and charitable activities throughout England and Scotland. The monks of Lindisfarne followed the old Celtic rites and practices, but Aidan traveled widely on the Continent and was able to familiarize them somewhat with the practices of the Roman Church, thus preparing his people for things to come.

Aidan trained a whole generation of Christian leaders for the English Church. Included among them were numerous bishops and saints. Perhaps the highest compliment paid to Aidan was that of the Venerable Bede who wrote that Aidan "taught no otherwise than he and his followers lived; for he neither sought nor loved anything of this world, but delighted in distributing to the poor whatsoever was given him by the kings or rich men of the world."

David Pendleton Oakerhater

Deacon

Cheyenne Brave Turned Servant of Christ

The Cheyenne brave called Oakerhater was an honored warrior in the cruel conflicts with white Americans that characterized the late 19th century. While being held as a prisoner of war at St. Augustine, Florida, he was converted to Christ. When he was released, he was baptized, taking the name David Pendleton, and studied for holy orders in Central New York. In 1881 he was ordained deacon and returned to his tribe in the Indian Territory, accompanied by his mentor, the Rev. John Wicks.

Oakerhater addressed his former comrades-in-arms, "...You remember when I led you out to war I went first and what I told you was true. Now, I have been away to the East and I have learned about another captain, the Lord Jesus Christ, and He is my Leader. He goes first, and all He tells me is true. I come back to my people to tell you to go with me now on this new road, into a war that makes peace..."

Many former warriors took up the cross. Father Wicks had to retire from missionary work in 1884 because of ill health, but Oakerhater continued, winning hundreds to Christ and earning the title among his people of "God's Warrior" and "Peace Chief." His establishment of the Whirlwind School near Fay, Oklahoma, was a landmark in the education and reconciliation of the Cheyenne. For nearly half a century David Pendleton Oakerhater was a tower of strength and a symbol of the new faith to his Native American brethren.

The Martyrs of New Guinea

Witnesses in World War II

New Guinea was the scene of much suffering when the Japanese invaded in 1942, especially among Christians there. Many European clergy and missionaries of other denominations had been withdrawn, had chosen to leave, or been forced to leave before the invasion. The Anglican Bishop of New Guinea, Philip Strong, issued this compelling message to his clergy: "We must endeavour to carry on or work. . . . God expects this of us. The church at home, which sent us out, will surely expect it of us. The universal church expects it of us. . . . The people whom we serve expect it of us. We could never hold up our faces again if, for our own safety, we all forsook him and fled, when the shadows of the passion began to gather around him in his spiritual and mystical body, the Church in Papua."

They stayed. Almost immediately there were arrests. Eight clergymen and two laymen were executed, "as an example." It was an example, indeed, and one which is well remembered, especially on September 2 in Australia and Indonesia. It was only the beginning of suffering and persecution which the young Church in New Guinea endured. It was the testing, the baptism in blood, which proved the metal of that young and vigorous part of Christ's Body.

Grant us, too, the courage to witness to our faith.

Constance and Companions

Angels of Mercy in a Time of Plague

Late in the summer of 1878 yellow fever struck Memphis, Tennessee, killing thousands. The Episcopal cathedral, St. Mary's, and its adjacent Church Home were in the center of the most infected area and became shelters for victims. The cathedral staff and the Sisters of St. Mary, who operated the Church Home, faced enormous burdens in caring for the sick and dying. Sisters on retreat in Peekskill, New York, when the epidemic broke out, instead of keeping a safe distance, rushed back to Memphis.

Sister Constance was the first of the nuns to be stricken with the fever. As she died on September 9 her last words were "Alleluia, Hosanna," simple words of praise that would ring in the ears of the people of Memphis for generations. They were subsequently inscribed on the high altar of the cathedral.

Sister Constance's companions in service to the sick and dying, Sisters Thecla and Ruth, soon followed her to the grave, as did Sister Frances, headmistress of the Church Home. She had nursed some thirty children at one time and had watched twenty-two die. Father Louis Schuyler, a chaplain to the Sisters of St. Mary, also died of the fever, as did Canon Charles Parsons. Canon Parsons was blessed with a vision of heaven as he lay dying and his last words were, "Lord Jesus, receive my spirit."

On this day we honor these, our companions in Christ, who gladly risked their own lives in order to save the lives of many and to assuage the final suffering of others.

John Henry Hobart

Bishop of New York

American Church Leader

Bishop Hobart, always a powerhouse of energy, was one of the most capable and effective leaders of any sort in America in the early 19th century. A native of Philadelphia, he was educated and taught at Princeton University prior to entering the Christian priesthood. After serving for sometime as Rector of Trinity Church, New York, he was elected Bishop of New York in 1811. Always full of vigor and excitement, he took the lackadaisical and self-satisfied diocese and transformed it into a dynamic and effective center of American church life.

Hobart was a tireless traveler, lecturer, and author, as well as being a staunch advocate of Episcopal polity and the *Book of Common Prayer*. He organized one of the most impressive missionary efforts the American Church has ever seen. Episcopal Churches began springing up in Western New York and among the American Indians, thanks largely to his work and inspiration. Always an educator, Hobart was largely responsible for the success of the college which bears his name today in Geneva, New York, and for the General Theological Seminary in New York City.

But above all, John Henry Hobart was a well loved and loving bishop, highly personable and always accessible. He set an example for the new American episcopate which is still worthy of emulation today.

We thank you for your servant John, faithful steward.

Cyprian

Died September 13, 258

Bishop of Carthage

Theologian, Pastor, and Martyr

Cyprian was a respected attorney of Carthage who converted to Christianity in middle age. He had been baptized only two years before he was consecrated Bishop of Carthage. When the Decian persecution broke out he fled under duress, but retained the respect of his flock, continuing to correspond with those who were riding out the persecution in the city. When the persecution subsided Cyprian returned to carefully and firmly rebuild the diocese.

When a plague broke out in 252 he quickly mobilized the church to help those in need and spent countless hours personally ministering to the sick of the city. This did not prevent public opinion and the authorities from blaming the plague on the "impious Christians." Soon there was another persecution. This time under the Emperor Valerian, and this time Bishop Cyprian chose to stay in the city. He was arrested and exiled for a time, then tried and finally executed. At the trial, Cyprian the lawyer clearly showed through in his deportment and courtesy before the pro-consul. He never displayed any hostility towards the court at all and he even left a generous tip for the executioner who chopped off his head.

Cyprian wrote a number of short treatises on Christian living, all of which show a profound understanding of human nature. He was a moderate and compassionate pastor and an example to his flock.

Holy Cross Day

The Exaltation of the Cross of Christ

"I, if I be lifted up, will draw all men unto me." It seemed in the 4th century that these words of Jesus were swiftly being fulfilled. Christianity had swept over the known, civilized world. A Christian Emperor now reigned from the throne of the Caesars and it was he, Constantine the Great, who, on this day in 335 A.D., dedicated the Church of the Holy Sepulcre in Jerusalem as a monument to the triumph of the Lord over the grave. This day was celebrated throughout Christendom as the feast of the lifting-up of the Cross of Christ over all the world.

The hope that the time was at hand when all men would acknowledge the Lordship of the Saviour was premature. But this dream has never been forgotten. Christian people still work and pray for the time when all men everywhere will return to their Creator, the Crucified and Risen Lord. This is a day for rejoicing in that hope, as Abraham rejoiced in looking forward to Christ's coming, though he had only the most vague notion of what it would be like. We look forward with joyful anticipation to the day when all men shall find their Lord, and we work toward making him known in every corner of his creation.

O God, who by the passion of your blessed Son has made his shameful death to be unto us the sign of life and peace: Grant us so to glory in the Cross of Christ, that we may gladly suffer shame and loss.

Ninian

Apostle

Died September 16, c.430

Bishop in Galloway

Ninian was the son of a British chieftain and a Christian. He was educated in Rome and a personal friend of Martin of Tours. He resolved to convert the fierce tribes of southern Scotland to Christianity and eventually had some success in so doing.

Ninian established a monastery at Whithorn called "Candida Casa" (i.e. "White House"). The abbey church came to be called St. Martin's, after the friend of Ninian. The monastery at Whithorn became a center for missionary and charitable activities throughout that portion of southern Scotland commonly called Galloway.

Otherwise, we know practically nothing of Ninian. This is as much due to his success and popularity as to anything else, for the story of his life has been so glossed over and glorified by later admirers that it is impossible to separate fact from fancy. The student of history is confronted with a barrage of fascinating legends, some preposterous, some perhaps embellished truth, all praising the beloved apostle of Galloway.

O God, you have caused the light of gospel to shine in the land of Britain through your servant Ninian: Grant, we beseech you, that having his life and labours in remembrance, we may show forth our thankfulness unto you for the same by following the example of his zeal and patience; through Jesus Christ our Lord.

Edward Bouverie Pusey

A Rich Man who entered the Kingdom of God

The friends of Forward Movement Publications may take pleasure in recalling that one of the most dynamic religious revivals in church history began with the publication of a series of pamphlets entitled "Tracts for the Times." One of the authors of these tracts was Edward Bouverie Pusey, an Oxford professor and priest in the Church of England. Dr. Pusey contributed to this religious revival, called the "Oxford Movement," not only as a teacher and writer, but also as one of the greatest preachers of his day.

A product of the English aristocracy, he exercised a sound and effective pastoral ministry to many of the Victorian upper class who were inclined to take a dilettante attitude towards religion. He was distressed by the church's failure to minister to the poor of the great cities and devoted most of his family's fortune to develop such ministries. He was instrumental in the founding of the Society of St. John the Evangelist, Oxford, and the Sisterhood of the Holy Cross, London. Working with the indefatigable foundress of the Society of the Most Holy Trinity, Mother Lydia Sellon, he assisted in the creation of an impressive array of charitable institutions for orphans and free trade schools for very poor boys and girls.

He never lost sight of the Catholic character of the Church of England and when his friend, John Henry Newman, defected to the Roman Church he became the principal leader of the Anglo-Catholic revival.

Theodore of Tarsus

Archbishop of Canterbury

Organizer of the English Church

The 7th century was not an age of international under-standing and communication. However, the church clearly thought of itself as one world-wide body. In 668 an African monk recommended to Pope Vitalian of Rome that he dispatch Theodore, a Greek whose home-town was Tarsus (in modern Turkey), to England to fill the vacant See of Canterbury. And so it was done.

Theodore turned out to be one of the most brilliant and effective Archbishops England ever had. He visited all of England and secured the unity of the Christian people of the land under the leadership of Canterbury, generations before any leaders of state could accomplish such a thing. He called two important councils of the English Church, one at Hertford and one at Hatfield, which ratified the orthodoxy and unity of the Church of England. He was tolerant of local traditions as long as they did not generate heresy or schism.

Theodore was an exceptionally well-educated and cosmopolitan individual. He is said to have written much, but, unfortunately, his scholarly work was little appreciated in primitive England and none of it survives to this day. His monument is the Church of England: catholic, orthodox, and unified.

O God, raise up in your church good and faithful stew-ards of the mysteries of Christ, as you did in thy servant Theodore.

105

John Coleridge Patteson

Died September 20, 1871

Bishop of Melanesia

And his Companions, Martyrs of the South Seas

All the Christian world was shocked to learn of the murder of good Bishop Patteson by natives on the Island of Nukapu in the South Pacific.

Patteson had been among the flowers of England's youth. He was educated at Eton and at Oxford University. He had rejected a promising and comfortable career in England and had given himself utterly to the task of civilizing and Christianizing the native peoples of Polynesia and Melanesia. For nearly twenty years he had served patiently and unselfishly, founding schools, hospitals, and churches, teaching, preaching and giving the sacraments to the natives of those lands. He also sought out and ministered to British settlers in those areas. He once presented the entire population of Pitcairn Island for confirmation, following the reconciliation of the *Bounty* mutineers with the British Government.

He was seriously concerned about the wanton practice of "blackbirding" or slave raiding which went on in the islands and was working vigorously to stop it. Nukapu had recently been victimized by such raiders and it was for this reason that Patteson's missionary ship, "The Southern Cross," anchored off that Island on this day in 1871 and the Bishop went ashore. He was killed that night by some of those whom he was trying to serve.

106

Sergius

Abbot of Holy Trinity, Moscow

Hero of Christian Russia

In Sergius' youth the Christians of Russia were suffering under the "Tartar Yoke," dominated and oppressed by pagan invaders. The Christian community was weak, divided, and confused. Under the vigorous leadership of Sergius and the monks of Holy Trinity monastery, they gained new hope. Sergius is best remembered as the beloved abbot who inspired Dmitri, Prince of Moscow, to resist Tartar domination. Equally important were his efforts to reform and revive the Russian Orthodox monasteries. He personally supervised the founding of over forty new monasteries.

Sergius is usually associated with the armed resistance to the Tartars, but he was also a great peace maker. He was often successful in mediating disputes among princes and on four occasions he averted civil war. Sergius was a man of deep faith and strong character. He was peasant born, hearty, neighborly, and practical. He struggled to keep the communal spirit alive among his monks and among the Christian people of Russia. He taught, by word and deed, absolute devotion to Christ as known in the Holy Eucharist and unselfish service to others.

Almighty and everlasting God, we give you thanks for the purity and strength with which you did endow your servant Sergius; and we pray that by your grace we may have a like power to hallow and confirm our souls.

Lancelot Andrewes

Died September 26, 1626

Bishop of Winchester

Scholar, Preacher, Pastor of 17th Century England

One of the brightest lights of 17th century England was Lancelot Andrewes, beloved pastor to the court of King James I and as fine a preacher as ever mounted the pulpit of St. Paul's, London. Andrewes, a Cambridge graduate, was a tireless and accurate scholar, the master of some fifteen languages. Perhaps the best Hebraist of his day, he was chiefly responsible for translating the Old Testament of the King James Version of the Bible.

As a young clergyman, his eloquent and erudite preaching attracted the attention of Queen Elizabeth, who offered him the great bishopric of Salisbury and later of Ely. He declined both, but accepted the position of Dean of Westminster. Finally, his well loved friend, King James I, persuaded him to take episcopal orders. He is best remembered as the saintly Bishop of Winchester.

He had profound insight into human nature and compassion for human weakness. He was a versatile and liberal pastor and had little use for the harshness and austerity of Calvinism, so popular in the British Isles in his day.

Lancelot Andrewes' lengthy sermons are far too academic for modern ears, but his book, *Private Devotions,* still enjoys perennial popularity.

Help us to follow the good examples of your servant Lancelot, and of all those who loved and served you.

Jerome

Died September 30, 420

Priest and Monk of Bethlehem

Theologian and Translator of Scripture

Jerome is chiefly remembered as the translator of the most famous and widely used version of the Bible ever published, the Latin Vulgate. In the 5th century most people in Western Europe spoke Latin, yet there was not an accurate or complete Latin text of the Bible. Jerome translated the entire Bible into Latin from its original Hebrew and Greek. He translated the sacred text into the common "street language" of his day, called "vulgar" Latin. In time this work came to be regarded as a "classic," but when it was published it was the subject of considerable controversy. Jerome deliberately did not use the elevated "Ciceronian" Latin with which he was so familiar, because he was warned in a dream that he was becoming a "Ciceronian and not a Christian."

A native of Strido, Italy, Jerome traveled widely and was educated in Rome, Antioch, Jerusalem, and Alexandria. He got envolved in practically every important issue of his day and was one of the most vehement adversaries of the Arian and Pelagian heresies. His correspondence reflects a strong faith and a sound mind as well as a passion for truth and integrity. He settled finally in Bethlehem as the head of a monastic community. One of history's greatest scholars and translators became a great pastor. "Now," he said, "we have to translate the words of scripture into deeds!"

Remigius

Died October 1, c.530

Bishop of Rheims

Apostle of the Franks

We know very little of Remigius (sometimes "Remi"). He lived in an age of relative obscurity. However, two startling events punctuate his biography and have assured his lasting fame.

First, he was consecrated Bishop of Rheims at age 22. In some times and places the consecration of one so young might be simply a reflection of the decadent politics of the church. In Remigius' case he seems to have been elected because of the genuine esteem in which he was held.

Second, he converted and baptised Clovis, the first Christian King of France. Remigius was a tireless missionary among the pagan Franks, and this event, which probably took place in 496, was the crowning achievement of his life.

Remigius was credited with a number of miracles and was perhaps the greatest preacher of France in his day. Through Remigius the light of the gospel shone forth in a dark and savage land and a new age and civilization was born: Christian France.

O God, the light of the faithful and shepherd of souls, who did call your servant Remigius to feed your sheep by his word, and guide them by his example: Grant us, we pray you, to keep the faith which he taught, and to follow in his footsteps; through Jesus Christ our Lord.

Francis of Assisi

Died October 4, 1226

Friar

Brother of the Poor

One of the boldest and most spirited figures in history, it is a shame that Francis is sometimes dimissed as simply a quiet "bird-watcher." Actually he was an outspoken and controversial "social activist." He was one of the greatest preachers of all time. His concern with poverty and ecology give him a strikingly modern quality. Although he was a wealthy cloth merchant's son, he gave all he had to help the poor and was contented with only the barest necessities for himself. He vigorously opposed the abuse of political power, particularly when it was wielded by the Bishop of Rome.

Francis was effective in initiating sweeping social and economic reforms. He was a popular singer, often called "God's Troubadour." His most famous hymn, "Canticle to Brother Sun" (307 in *The Hymnal 1940*), has stood the test of time. Francis founded one of the strongest and most dynamic religious orders in Christendom. Today we find Franciscan Friars in both the Roman and Anglican communions.

Most high, almighty, and good Lord: Grant your people grace to renounce gladly the vanities of this world, that, after the example of blessed Francis, we may for love of you delight in all your creatures, with perfectness of joy; through Jesus Christ our Lord.

William Tyndale

Priest

Scholar and Translator of the Bible

Change, even the most innocent and constructive, comes hard to men and societies. When William Tyndale, a careful and competent scholar and priest, prepared a translation of the Bible into English, he suddenly found himself treated as a scoundrel and a radical, even by those from whom he had expected the most support, the intellectuals and churchmen of England.

At Oxford, as a student, and at Cambridge, as a teacher, he had found great truth and guidance for his life from the scriptures, which were then available only to those who could read Latin, or in the partial and sometimes inaccurate version of John Wyclif. Tyndale wanted to make the Bible available to Englishmen in their native tongue. When his bishop got word of the project, he chastised Tyndale for such "revolutionary" activity and eventually made things so uncomfortable for the scholar that he had to leave England and flee to Germany, where the first edition of the Tyndale Version of the Bible was published.

In spite of Tyndale's piety, scholarship, and good intentions, his work brought nothing but wrath from the English authorities. He was captured, tried as a heretic and schismatic, strangled, and publicly burned at Vilvorde, Belgium, in 1536.

We thank you, Lord, for the constancy and zeal of your servant William.

Robert Grosseteste

Bishop of Lincoln

Great Pastor, Reformer, and Scholar

Had the leaders of the 13th century paid more attention to this wise and devout pastor and scholar, many of the disasters of the next three centuries might have been avoided. Robert was a very bright peasant lad from Suffolk, England, who was educated by the church at Oxford and Paris. His charm, intellect, and piety gained the attention of the authorities and he was made Rector of Oxford and eventually consecrated Bishop of Lincoln. In that position his chief concern was for the welfare of his flock, both spiritually and temporally. He visited all the churches in the diocese and quickly relieved many of the prominent clergy because they were neglecting their pastoral duties. He staunchly opposed the corrupt practice of the Bishop of Rome of making Italian priests absentee clergy for English churches. He insisted that his priests spend their time in the service of their people, in prayer, and in study. He went on a pilgrimage to Rome where he spoke out boldly against many of the corruptions of the church. His sermons were moving and prophetic, but they went unheeded by the Papacy.

Back in England, where he was welcomed as a hero, he witnessed the signing of the Magna Carta, which he firmly supported, and continued his inexhaustable quest for knowledge, writing, studying and teaching astronomy, philosophy, optics, physics, poetry, and Holy Scripture. Grosseteste was a man of piety, integrity, courage, and compassion.

Teresa of Avila

Died October 14, 1582

Nun

Mystic and Foundress

Undisciplined mystics sometimes become so enthralled in their rapturous experiences, so "heavenly minded," that they are "of no earthly use." A sterling example of a more othodox and incarnational mystic piety is found in Teresa of Avila, a Spanish contemplative who found time to lead reforms, found a major religious order (the Discalced Carmelites), write a number of excellent books and engage in countless charitable activities and in theological dialogue with some of the best minds of her day.

Although a deeply spiritual and intuitive person, she resisted the temptation to dismiss the rational, analytical and practical. Her powerful mystic experiences with God led her to love, not reject, humankind, and to hope, not despair, concerning human history. Her confidence in God's love and grace for all gave her a sparkling optimism and good humor which enabled her to minister to the heirs of the Renaissance in ways that the more dour and world-rejecting theologians of her day could not. Her brutally honest and deeply insightful autobiographical writings caused Frederich Heiler to call her a modern "psychologist among the saints." Her openness to change and her reforming spirit raised the suspicions of the Inquisition and she found herself the center of much controversy.

Her most famous pupil was John of the Cross. Her most famous book is *The Interior Castle*.

Samuel Isaac Joseph Schereschewsky

Bishop of Shanghai

Apostle to the Chinese

It is hard to imagine a more cosmopolitan and ecumenical character than Samuel Schereschewsky, a Lithuanian Jew, trained in a Rabbinic school in Poland, an imigrant to America, baptised by a Baptist minister and educated in Presbyterian and Episcopalian seminaries. He went to China as a missionary in the service of the Episcopal Church and was eventually consecrated Bishop of Shanghai.

He was a robust and active man whose life style was severely disrupted when he suffered from a stroke which incapacitated him and forced his return to America. For the rest of his life he was confined to a wheelchair. Undaunted, it was in this condition that he did his most famous work. Always an excellent linguist, he now gave his full attention to the translation of the entire Bible into two chinese dialects. Eventually it was necessary for him to return to China where Chinese scribes could complete the details of this monumental work. Leaving China for the last time, he was taken to Japan where the American Bible Society was publishing his work and there he died. The trip had, presumably, been too much for his old and exhausted frame. The Lord had given vast and inscrutable China an apostle worthy of her nature and dignity.

115

Hugh Latimer and Nicholas Ridley

Died October 16, 1555

Bishops

Reformers and Martyrs

"Today we shall light such a fire in England as shall never be extinguished." With these words Latimer and Ridley went to the stake and were burned to death on this day in 1555 at Oxford.

Besides being burned together, Latimer and Ridley had much in common. Both were English Bishops with strong Protestant sympathies. Each was an exceptionally fine preacher in an age of great preachers. Both were Cambridge men. Both were social reformers.

Latimer was the sometime Bishop of Worcester, who first rose to prominence in the days of Thomas Cardinal Wolsey and Henry VIII. In those days he was one of only twelve priests licensed to preach anywhere in England. He first gained a reputation as a social reformer and then as a church reformer. This alone was enough to put Queen Mary on his heels.

Nicholas Ridley, the sometime Bishop of London, was equally infamous to Mary's "bloody" inquisitors. During his brief episcopate he had seen to the founding of three hospitals and had contributed significantly to the new *Book of Common Prayer*. His "Protestantizing" sermons brought down upon his head the wrath of Mary's most unreconciliatory regime.

Yet Latimer and Ridley had, indeed, lit a fire in England that was not to be extinguished.

Thomas Cranmer
Archbishop of Canterbury

English Reformer

As Archbishop of Canterbury during the reigns of both Henry VIII and Edward VI, Cranmer presided over the reform of the Church of England. He was the chief composer of the *Book of Common Prayer* and contributed significantly to the translation of the *Bible* into English. He was one of the foremost scholars of his day, an eminent student of the Holy Scripture and the Liturgy.

Cranmer was convinced that a thorough reform of the church was needed in his day. He was a staunch opponent of the Papacy and one of those who declared the "Bishop of Rome hath no more authority in England than any other foreign bishop." However, he accepted episcopal orders and he did not favour the total dissolution of the monasteries.

When Mary Tudor, called "Bloody Mary" in English folklore, ascended the throne, Cranmer was imprisoned and convicted of heresy. For this he was burned at the stake at Oxford on March 21, 1556. Prior to the execution he had, under duress, signed recantations repudiating his reforming activities. For this he publicly repented and at the stake he is said to have willfully placed his right hand into the flames, saying, "This hand hath offended." His dying day was the noblest of his life.

Praise God for Cranmer and all martyrs and reformers in all ages.

Ignatius

Died October 17, c.115

Bishop of Antioch

Bishop and Martyr

When the Roman Emperor, Trajan, ordered that Ignatius, Bishop of Antioch, be brought to Rome for public execution as an "atheist and subversive," he made a serious blunder. The journey which Ignatius was compelled to take was long and calls were made at numerous ports. Few men were unimpressed by the sight of the saintly old bishop being hauled in chains to his death. Crowds of Christians and Christian sympathizers gathered at his ports of call to cheer him on. Others joined him and helped record and distribute his letters which soon became famous. In these letters Ignatius rejoiced at his opportunity to witness for Christ through martyrdom. He warned Christians against the grave danger of heresy within their ranks and urged them to follow the teaching and practice of their duly elected and consecrated bishops. He was one of the first important literary defenders of the three-fold ministry: bishops, priests, and deacons.

Ignatius' letters to the Christians in Ephesus, Magnesia, Trolles, Rome, Philadelphia, and Smyrna, are among our most valuable documents of the early church. He was brutally put to death before a mob in the Colosseum at Rome, but the testimony of his life and letters lived on to inspire his fellows in Christ.

We thank you for your servant Ignatius who triumphed over suffering and despised death.

118

Henry Martyn

Priest

Missionary to India and Persia

One good example is worth a thousand exhortations. The good example of young Henry Martyn lead to a flurry of enthusiasm for the Church of England's missionary efforts in India and the East.

Martyn was born in Truro, England, and educated at Cambridge, where he was a friend of Chaplain Simeon. Henry was a very bright, lovable, and dedicated young man, and it was probably Simeon who encouraged him to take up a missionary vocation. In 1805 Martyn became a chaplain for the East India Company, upon Simeon's recommendation, and sailed to India. There he served the Church in Calcutta, founded schools at Patna and Cawnpore, and translated the New Testament and the Book of Common Prayer into Hindustani. He traveled widely, preaching, teaching, and helping those in need in every way he could.

He went to Persia and there translated the New Testament into Persian. Travel in those days brought few pleasures and many hazards. Exhausted and seeking some respite for soul and body he went into Asia Minor where the climate and civilization were somewhat more hospitable. There, at Tokat (in modern Turkey), he became very ill and was befriended by Armenian Christians. He died there at age 31 and buried by Armenian clergy.

We thank you, Lord, for Henry and all missionaries.

James of Jerusalem

Brother of Jesus, Apostle and Martyr

James was, according to the Gospels of Matthew and Mark, and according to Paul, a brother of Jesus. Yet, he was not a believer during the Lord's earthly ministry. Jesus appeared to him after the resurrection and he was converted.

He soon rose to prominence in the church and became the Bishop of Jerusalem. He presided over the important Council in Jerusalem which decided to permit Gentiles to join the church. As the church grew and prospered, he became less and less popular with the authorities. According to the highly reliable historian, Josephus, he was eventually stoned and clubbed to death by a mob.

James of Jerusalem is usually considered to be the author of the Epistle of James. If this is the case, he certainly had a clear insight into the Lord's message and ministry and its relationship to the Old Covenant.

Grant, we pray, O God, that after the example of your servant James, the brother of our Lord, your Church may give itself continually to prayer, and to the reconciliation of all who are at variance and enmity; through Jesus Christ our Lord, who lives and reigns with you in the unity of the Holy Spirit, one God, now and for ever.

Note: *Forward Day by Day* is a manual of daily Bible readings and devotions, issued quarterly.

Alfred the Great

Died October 26, 899

King of Wessex

A Christian Prince in a Savage Land

In the "Dark Ages," when much of Britain was yet un-Christianized and uncivilized, there arose among the West Saxons in Southern England a great king, who was an example of piety and learning. Alfred the Great was wise and courageous and used his temporal power for the spiritual, intellectual, and economic advancement of his people.

In his youth, Alfred knew the terror of mortal illness, of invasion, and of the death of loved ones. In the savage warfare of his day he was brave, strong, and cunning. He was not a man unacquainted with grief and hardship or unfamiliar with the harsh realities of life. From the monks of Wessex and from his teachers in Rome, he learned a kinder, gentler, nobler way of life than most of his people had even been exposed to, although they were at least nominally Christian. When, in his maturity, he became the most powerful of the Anglo-Saxon Kings, he administered justice with insight and fairness, laying the foundation for much of the best in English law. He founded a palace school which was unequaled in Northern Europe.

He is well remembered in stone at his capital city, Winchester, and well commemorated in modern leaders who truly seek the moral, physical, and intellectual betterment of their people. King Alfred the Great was in fact what King Arthur was to become in fancy; the model Christian King.

James Hannington

Died October 29, 1885

Bishop of Eastern Equatorial Africa

Missionary and Martyr

James Hannington was one of those Englishmen who caught a vision of what needed to be done on "the Dark Continent" and set out to offer all he could in service for Africa's people. He served for a time as a missionary priest in Eastern Africa, but had to return to England because of ill health. In 1884 he went back to Africa, having recovered, carrying with him episcopal orders. He was enthroned at Mombasa and set out to establish a series of mission stations west to Lake Victoria Nyanza by way of Mount Kilimanjaro. A new king had just ascended the throne in Uganda and when he heard of Bishop Hannington's approach he feared it was an attack on his kingdom and dispatched warriors to eliminate the problem. Hannington and his companions soon found themselves surrounded by hostile warriors. A group of them encircled the bishop and paused before plunging their spears into him just long enough for him to say his last words, "Go tell your king that I die for the people of Buganda, and that I have purchased the road to Uganda with my life." Within the next few days many of the native Christians of the area were brutally tortured and martyred.

But the story did not end there. The church prevailed and today thrives among the natives of Uganda, Rwanda, and Burundi.

Bless all who serve in the land of Africa as witnesses.

Commemoration of All Faithful Departed

A Cloud of Witnesses

If we have trouble thinking of dear old Aunt Polly or Uncle John as being "saints," now is the appropriate time to formally remember them. There are countless departed souls who were faithful Christians but who could hardly be regarded as exemplary "saints." We like to remember them and to give thanks to God publicly for them.

This occasion, sometimes called "All Souls Day," is a twin feast of "All Saints Day." It has been observed in the Eastern Church from very early times and was introduced into Western Europe in the 10th century. The 16th century English Reformers cut this festival out of the Church Year because they did not like to distinguish between "all saints" and "all souls." The New Testament makes no such distinction but, rather, refers to all Christians as saints, stressing the fact that salvation is a gift from God and that none of us earns a special place in his kingdom by our good deeds. This is a good time to remember the unspectacular children of God; those whose Christian witness may have been weak or faltering, but who are still very dear and important to God and to us.

O God, who has brought us near to an innumerable company of Angels, and to the spirits of just men made perfect: Grant us during our pilgrimage to abide in their fellowship, and to become partakers of their joy.

Richard Hooker

Priest

Anglican Theologian

The master theologian of the English Reformation, Richard Hooker, was a relatively obscure person in his own day. His famous tome, *The Laws of Ecclesiastical Polity,* was a landmark in English literature, philosophy, and churchmanship. There has never been a more thorough and convincing apologist for Anglicanism, yet we know little of his life. He was an Oxford graduate and served several relatively undistinguished parishes during his somewhat short ministry (he seems to have died at age 46).

Some of his basic positions and arguments are so familiar to modern Episcopalians as to seem almost like cliches. He argued for the reasonable and reverent use of Holy Scripture, rejecting the Roman Catholic disregard for scripture and the Puritan's literal and mechanical view of it. He saw the church as a living organism, rather like a family, and not as a static and impersonal institution that could never change, nor as a purely "spiritual" and intellectual association of subscribers.

It would certainly do violence to Hooker's own teaching if modern Episcopalians regarded him as the definitive teacher and final authority. But one can say that Richard Hooker best expressed, intellectually, the mind and spirit of 17th century Anglicanism.

Enrich us by the teaching of your servant Richard.

Willibrord

Archbishop of Utrecht

Apostle to Holland

Willibrord is one of the most celebrated of the Anglo-Saxon saints of the early Middle Ages. He was highly praised by both the Venerable Bede and Alcuin of York, the major historians of that period. He was a native of Northumbria, England, and a student of Wilfred, famous Bishop of Northumbria. He was ordained a priest in Ireland where he studied under some the best Christian teachers of Britain.

After an arduous, but successful, pilgrimage to Rome, Willibrord set out, with the blessing of the Bishop of Rome, to convert the fierce and pagan Frisians of what is today called the Netherlands or Holland. The details of that venture are not accurately recorded. We only know that it was highly successful. Willibrord established a strong and dedicated Christian "beachhead" at Utrecht, where he eventually became Archbishop.

Willibrord typifies a long standing relationship between English and Dutch Christians. Today the historic Diocese of Utrecht is in full communion with the Church of England.

O almighty God, who in your providence did choose your servant Willibrord to be an apostle to the Frisian people, to bring those who were wandering in darkness and error to the true light and knowledge of you: Grant us so to walk in that light, that we may come at last to the light of everlasting life.

Leo the Great

Bishop of Rome

Bishop and Statesman in the Dark Ages

Leo, Bishop of Rome, captured the imagination of generations of Europeans when he stood before the terrible horde of the Huns and persuaded them to withdraw to the Danube. He settled the most heated and dangerous theological dispute since Nicaea, when his legates ended the Eutychian controversy. He succeeded in getting imperial and ecclesiastical endorsement for his claim that the Bishop of Rome was primate of the Catholic Church in Western Europe. Leo the Great was a statesman par excellence and is sometimes called the "Founder of the Papacy." He appeared in a very troubled time in the "Dark Ages" of Western Europe and was a veritable saviour not only of the church but of law and order of any kind, indeed, of civilization.

Leo's most famous written work, his *Tome*, remains a classic statement of Christian doctrine. His sermons and letters still reveal to us a clear, forcible, and intelligent pastor, though not an unusually brilliant or profound one.

Almighty, everlasting God, whose servant Leo steadfastly confessed the true faith of your Son our Saviour Jesus Christ to be Very God and Very Man: Grant that we may hold fast to this faith, and evermore magnify his holy Name; through the same your Son Jesus Christ our Lord, who lives and reigns with you and the Holy Spirit ever, one God, world without end.

126

Martin

Died November 11, 397

Bishop of Tours

A Patron of Soldiers and of Justice

Martin was reared a pagan and became an officer in the Roman army. As a young officer serving in the Province of Gaul (France) he became an "inquirer" or catechumen of the Christian faith. At Amiens he encountered a beggar who was cold and naked. Moved with compassion he ripped his own officer's cloak in two and gave the beggar half. From that time on he resolved to become a Christian and follow the Lord's way of life.

After obtaining a discharge from the army, he traveled about a good deal but finally settled at Poitiers where he and Hilary, the Bishop of Poitiers, founded a religious community. Martin was eventually elected Bishop of Tours and in that capacity he became famous as a pastor and evangelist. He succeeded in establishing parishes and monasteries throughout the region. Martin was a strong advocate of justice in a time and place when power seemed to rule. He was indignant and protested any mistreatment of heretics or pagans by Christians, and vice versa.

Martin became a patron saint of France. He was also very popular among the old Celtic Christians of Britain. Augustine, the first Archbishop of Canterbury, was startled upon arriving at what he presumed to be pagan Britain, to find a Christian Church, St. Martin's, at Canterbury.

O Lord, may we, too, withstand the world's temptations.

Charles Simeon

Priest

Died November 12, 1836

Chaplain to Cambridge

Frequently, when a person has an overpowering and deeply personal religious experience he will turn away from the relatively cold, static, and worldly "institutional" church. This need not and should not be the case. Charles Simeon is a beautiful example of an evangelical Christian whose life was changed by a personal religious experience while an undergraduate, but who remained all his life a most loyal churchman. He always saw the church as his proper home and as a real vehicle of grace for all men. He was one of the foremost evangelical preachers of his day, yet remained, also, a staunch advocate of the *Book of Common Prayer* and of bishops. Although his position was reasonable, sound, and just, it exposed him to severe criticism from both the "High Church" and the "Evangelical" parties. He was ridiculed, insulted, and threatened with physical violence by one group and then by the other.

Charles Simeon spent his entire ministry as a chaplain at Cambridge University. There his academic ability, his talent as a preacher, and his genuine concern for people enabled him to exert a great influence for good on a generation of Cambridge men. He was an excellent student of the Bible and led many young men to discover the sacred book's relevance and message for their lives. He was one of the founders of the Church Missionary Society.

Samuel Seabury *Consecrated November 14, 1784*

Bishop of Connecticut

First American Bishop

On this day in 1784 the first American bishop was consecrated in Aberdeen, Scotland, in a quiet ceremony in the private chapel of Bishop John Skinner. In this way the episcopate was brought to America and it was possible for Americans to organize an episcopal church, independent of the Church of England. The English bishops could not legally consecrate an American bishop who would not swear allegiance to the English Crown and for this reason Seabury had to go to Scotland for episcopal orders. Soon the English laws were modified to allow for the consecration of American bishops in the English succession.

Samuel Seabury of Connecticut was a controversial figure and hardly conformed to the traditional idea of a "saint." Unlike our other early bishops, White of Pennsylvania, Provoost of New York, and Madison of Virginia, Seabury opposed the American Revolution. For this, and because he was considered terribly "high church" for the times, he was not generally popular. Yet he performed an invaluable service for the American Church in securing the episcopacy for her. Feelings ran high against bishops in those days, especially in New England. It took considerable courage and determination for him to go to England and Scotland and then return to Connecticut as a bishop.

Grant that we may serve you diligently in our day.

Margaret

Died November 16, 1093

Queen of Scotland

Exemplary Wife, Queen, and Mother

When the Normans successfully invaded England in 1066 the Anglo-Saxon royalty fled from England. Margaret, a cousin of the defeated king, fled with her mother and sister to Scotland where they found refuge in the court of the Scottish King Malcolm. Margaret soon married King Malcolm and became Scotland's most beloved and revered queen.

She was always a deeply religious person, showing great interest in the church and great compassion for the poor. In her youth she considered a religious vocation and in her maturity she found one, as wife and mother. Her firm and loving influence on the king, the church, her children, and the people, virtually renewed the life of the whole nation of Scotland. Under her influence monasteries, schools, orphanages, and hospitals were founded and the quality of life greatly improved in the land. One tragic aspect of Scottish life about which Margaret could do nothing was that of clan warfare and blood feuds. Malcolm was treacherously slain at Alnwick in 1093 and the grief-stricken Margaret died a few days later. Their son, David, became one of Scotland's finest kings. Their daughter, Matilda, married the English King Henry I and so Margaret and Malcolm are ancestors of the present British Royal Family.

As you did endue with zeal and charity your servant Margaret, so endue us.

Hugh

Bishop of Lincoln

A Bold and Beloved English Bishop

Hugh was as thoroughly attractive and virile a figure as ever graced the pages of English history. He was an able sportsman, a lover of children and of animals, an excellent administrator, and a man whose humor and kindness literally charmed the socks off the English court. Although a man of strong temper himself, Hugh was one of the very few who could calm the raging of King Henry II.

Hugh was a native of Avalon, Burgundy, in what is now France. He came to England as abbot of the Charterhouse monastery at Witham in Somerset. Later he was elected Bishop of Lincoln, then the largest diocese in England.

He was a vigorous opponent of injustice of any kind, a sort of ecclesiastical Robin Hood. He boldly supported the peasants in defiance of the king's harsh forest laws. On more than one occasion he faced, alone, rioting mobs, incensed against the Jews. He refused to allow the powerful and popular King Richard I to raid the church's treasury to support his crusades. If ever the title "prince of the church" was appropriate for a bishop, it was appropriate for Hugh of Lincoln.

O God, as your servant Hugh did feed your sheep by his word, and guide them by his example, so may we.

Abbess of Whitby

Grand Lady of the British Church

The lovely Hilda was like a breath of Spring in the dark winter of 7th century England. She was born of the pagan royalty of Northumbria. When she was thirteen years old her great uncle, King Edwin, was converted and she was baptised with his household. She was a lady of some rank and station and, although deeply touched by the new faith, hesitated to enter upon a religious vocation until she was over thirty. Eventually she founded a monastery herself at Whitby, with the help of Aidan, Bishop of Lindisfarne. The Whitby monastery was mixed, men and women, and became a great center of the old British Church. There, according to Bede, Hilda oversaw the careful teaching of Holy Scripture, "by word and example, righteousness and mercy and purity, and especially peace and charity." There the famous Anglo-Saxon poet, Caedmon, was befriended and there he composed much of his work. There in 664 King Oswy called the church council which decided on the Romanization of the old British (Celtic) Church. Hilda was not pleased with this decision which seriously changed the worship and discipline of her community. However, she gracefully accepted it, relinquishing local customs in the interest of the unity and order of the Universal Church.

O Lord, may we have a like power to hallow and conform our souls and bodies to your holy will.

Elizabeth

Princess of Hungary

Sister of the Unfortunate

Being born "with a silver spoon in one's mouth" does not assure security in life, and one's own generosity to others does not guarantee repayment in kind by others. Elizabeth was well born, the daughter of the King of Hungary, carefully reared and wisely married to the noble Landgrave of Thuringia, Germany. She was a loving and exemplary wife and mother. However, when she was only twenty years old, her husband was killed and she and her children became the wards of her husband's cruel and selfish brother, Henry Raspe. Eventually he expelled Elizabeth and her little ones from the family home, Wartburg Castle, and this in the dead of winter.

Elizabeth sought refuge in the church in Marburg, but even there she was not kindly treated. The stern, powerful, and insensitive priest, Conrad, called "the Master of Marburg," had her children taken from her and placed her in a convent of women Franciscans, "Poor Clares." There she was treated with almost sadistic severity. "Like grass beaten by a thunderstorm," to use her own phrase, she revived to become the most beloved "sister of the poor" of Marburg. She often sewed garments for poor children until her fingers bled, or went days without sleep caring for the sick. She met an early death and even old Conrad repented and acknowledged that he had, indeed, mistreated a saint.

133

Edmund

King

Anglo-Saxon Martyr

In 833 with the strong support of the Christian clergy, Edmund became King of East Anglia, one of the Anglo-Saxon kingdoms. By that time the Anglo-Saxons had been throughly Christianized and Edmund strove to be a model Christian king. He devoted himself to the worship of God, to learning and to the administration of justice and charity.

However, in 870 his little kingdom was overrun by an army of heathen Danes. They captured the King and offered him his life if he would accept Danish law and custom and if he would share authority with a pagan leader. He saw that such a compromise would result in injustice to his people, would further imperil the life of the church and dilute the character of his nation. He declined. The Danish soldiers stripped him and tied him to a tree. They whipped him and their archers used him for a target, torturing him by firing arrows into his limbs and nonvital parts of his body. Their sadistic orgy ended when their king finally ordered that Edmund's head be severed from his body.

He was buried at a place which came to be called Bury St. Edmunds. It became one of the principal shrines of medieval England and the site of a great Benedictine monastery. His life is a symbol of good Christian leadership in the secular realm and his death is a Christian witness of uncompromising integrity and fidelity.

134

Clement

Bishop of Rome

Pastor and Epistler of the Early Church

Clement was, as best we can determine, the third Bishop of Rome. He is believed to be the Clement mentioned in *Philippians 4:3* and he may well have known Paul and Peter personally. He was in all probability an ex-slave of the family of Titus Flavius Clemens, relatives of the Emperor Domitian. However, his fame rests primarily on a letter he wrote to the Christians in Corinth in about 95. It is usually called I Clement and has often been regarded as canonical scripture.

This beautiful epistle is an admonition to the Corinthian Christians to be patient with one another, to obey the legitimate church authorities and to concentrate on demonstrating to each other and to the world the wonderful love of Christ. "Let each man be subject to his neighbor," wrote Clement. "Let the strong care for the weak, and let the weak respect the strong. Let the rich provide for the poor, and let the poor give thanks that God has given him one to supply his need. Let the wise man show his wisdom, not in words, but in good deeds."

Clement's verses on love are second only to those of Paul himself. Also, like Paul, he builds a strong case for obedience to church leadership and admonishes against rebellious spirits, envy, jealousy, and strife.

O God, raise up faithful witnesses today, like Clement, who will set forth the truth of your salvation.

James Otis Sargent Huntington

Died November 25, 1935

Priest and Monk

Founder of the Order of the Holy Cross

He was the son of a bishop and a Harvard graduate. None of his contemporaries could have guessed that James Huntington would spend most of his life championing the poor and founding a religious community. As a young priest he first tried his vocation among the very poor of the Lower East Side of New York City. Eyebrows were raised among "proper" Episcopalians when he taught choirboys to sing "Our Lord He was a Carpenter" and many regarded it as downright scandalous when he joined the Knights of Labor.

In 1884 he founded a religious order for men called the Order of the Holy Cross. He wrote the order's rule and served as its Superior for many years. Attired in the habit of the order he led a demonstration in support of coal miners who were on strike in Streator, Illinois. But his mind turned constantly to learning and prayer. He founded St. Andrew's School for Mountain Boys in Tennessee and Kent School in Connecticut.

In 1904 he secured a permanent mother house at West Park, New York. He established a school for wayward girls in Connecticut and a mission in Liberia.

His last years were devoted mainly to prayer, contemplation and to the pastoral care of the order. He died at 84.

Kamehameha and Emma

King and Queen of Hawaii

Patrons of the Church in Hawaii

The Hawaiian Islands were first evangelized by sternly Calvinistic Congregationalists and by Roman Catholics. Neither group had much respect for the other or for the native Hawaiian culture and traditions. King Kamehameha IV, who was crowned in 1854, and his wife, Queen Emma, actively sought a branch of Christianity that was all-embracing, reconciliatory and accepting of Hawaiian culture, yet orthodox and traditional.

They found such in Anglicanism and were married by Anglican rites. Queen Victoria served as godmother to their son. Under royal patronage Thomas N. Staley became Hawaii's first bishop, ground was broken for St. Andrew's Cathedral in Honolulu, The Book of Common Prayer was translated into Hawaiian, the Queen's Hospital was founded and several schools were established in the islands with Anglican clergy as tutors.

Kamehameha was only twenty-nine when he died. Queen Emma lived on for many years and became a symbol of dignity and Christian piety to the people of Hawaii. The Archbishop of Canterbury described her as one of the most saintly souls he had ever met.

137

Nicholas Ferrar

Deacon

Died December 1, 1637

Founder of Little Gidding

Every generation of Christians seems to produce its own kind of religious community, from ancient Athos to modern Taize. Little Gidding in Huntingtonshire, England, was one of its generations most famous religious communities. Nicholas Ferrar was the founder and chaplain of Little Gidding.

He was well-born, well-educated, and well-traveled. Ferrar was a Member of Parliament and a trustee of the Virginia Company. When he was thirty-four years old he retired to his family estate at Little Gidding and, with a number of friends, organized a semi-monastic community of men and women. Members of the community followed a very strict rule of life, using the *Book of Common Prayer* for their guide. They did not take vows of celibacy and did not withdraw from the world. They were very active in providing for the poor, operating a free school and a hospital. Through three decades Little Gidding established and maintained an impeccable reputation for charity and godly living. However, the Puritans, at the height of their raging against the prayerbook and "popery," broke up the community, violently. They contemptuously called it a "protestant nunnery." When the Puritan tide ebbed and the church was restored in England, Little Gidding was not revived. However, its spirit of real Christian community and of service to human beings in need, is continually being renewed in the church.

Channing Moore Williams

Died December 2, 1910

Bishop of Japan

Missionary to the Chinese and Japanese

This quiet, shy, patient, and scholarly priest first entered Japan as a missionary in 1859 after several years experience in China. He was greeted as an "evil corrupter" and a "foreign devil." His only colleague, John Liggins, was severely beaten by a mob and had to return to America. Williams carried on in his inimitable way, and gradually gained the confidence of the Japanese.

He lived in stark simplicity, adopted a distinctly Japanese life style, and became a master of the Japanese language. Williams was a native of Virginia and the American Civil War brought great personal grief to him as well as a dearth of missionary funds. When peace came, he toured America, raising money for his work, was consecrated Bishop and returned to Japan. Gradually the Lord's work prospered.

St. Paul's University (Kyoto), St. Luke's Hospital (Tokyo), and numerous lesser institutions were started. Perhaps the greatest joy in William's life came with the organization of the Nippon Seikokai (The Holy Catholic Church in Japan) in 1886. On his gravestone some Japanese friends placed this touching epitaph, "During his fifty years in Japan he taught Christ's ways and not his own."

139

John of Damascus

Died December 4, c.760

Priest and Monk

Champion of Orthodox Christianity

The son of an important official in the court of the Moslem Caliph of Damascus, John had an easy rapport with the Moslems among whom he was reared and whom he regarded as simply heretical Christians. He readily succeeded to his father's office in the Caliph's court. Later, he abandoned the wealth and comfort of the fashionable life of Damascus and joined a religious community in Palestine.

As he lived the rigorous life of a monk in the stark wilderness near the Dead Sea, his own rich and strong personality began to emerge. He soon distinguished himself as a theologian and scholar. His chief published work extant is *The Fount of Knowledge*. He is recognized as a "Doctor of the Universal Church." However, John of Damascus is most widely remembered for his contributions to Christian worship. He wrote many fine hymns, including two Easter ones that are still popular today: "Come ye faithful raise the strain . . ." and "The Day of Resurrection, earth tell it out abroad!" He effectively defended the doctrine of the Real Presence in the Eucharist, the veneration of the Lord's Mother, and use of sacred pictures, "icons." In the latter he became envolved in an international religio-political struggle called the "Iconoclastic Controversy" which reached violent proportions and shook the Byzantine world. His life was saved in this controversy by his powerful Moslem friends.

Clement of Alexandria

Died December 5, c.210

Priest

Early Scholar and Apologist

Titus Flavius Clement was a sophisticated Greek, well educated in philosophy and well traveled. He was converted to Christianity largely through the efforts of Pantaenus, the head of a Christian school in Alexandria, Egypt. Unlike some of his contemporaries, Clement was not at all willing to leave his philosophical training at the baptismal font. He found Christianity to be quite compatible with philosophy and he continued to practice and refine his speculative skills. He regarded Socrates and Plato as important forerunners of Christ, asserting that their teaching prepared men to accept and understand the gospel much as the Old Testament prophets had.

His extant works include: *An Exhortation to the Greeks* and *Instruction in Christian Living*. For most of his adult life his home was Alexandria, with its renowned library and university. Clement served as principal of the Christian school there. However, he also visited the Christian communities in Antioch and Jerusalem, where he was highly regarded. He died under unknown circumstances during the persecution of the Emperor Septimus Severus.

O God, who has enlightened your Church by the teaching of your servant Clement: Enrich us evermore, we beseech you, with your heavenly grace, and raise up faithful witnesses to the truth of your salvation.

Nicholas

Died December 6, c.342

Bishop of Myra

Protector of Children and Sailors

It is no wonder that in England, a country so concerned about her children and her navy, more churches have been named in honor of Nicholas than for any other saint. He was the Bishop of Myra in what is now Turkey.

Tradition has it that he was a nobleman who poured out his fortune to care for poor children. Countless legends surround his deeds of kindness to sailors. Dutch settlers in New Amsterdam called him "Santa Claus." His costume and his image have been secularized and his beloved ships have been replaced by, of all things, reindeer. But, his spirit of love for children remains.

Clement Clarke Moore, a devoted churchman and professor at the General Theological Seminary in New York, has left us a pleasant bit of fantasy called "A Visit From St. Nicholas" which begins, "Twas the night before Christmas. . . ." Around the world at Christmas time St. Nicholas will not be forgotten in song and ceremony, but those who honor him best are those who honor his Lord and who work continually for the care and protection of children.

Almighty and everlasting God, who did enkindle the flame of your love in the heart of your servant Nicholas: Grant to us, your humble servants, the same faith and power of love; that, as we rejoice in his triumph, we may profit by his example.

Ambrose

Died December 7, 397

Bishop of Milan

A Father of the Western Church

Ambrose was born of a prominent and powerful Roman family and at the time he was acclaimed Bishop of Milan he was an important Roman official, but had not yet been baptised! He accepted the Christian faith and the office of bishop in virtually the same breath. He had been studying to become a Christian but on the day he was elected bishop he had entered the cathedral only as a ruler of state interested in quelling the violent conflict between the Arians and the orthodox Christians.

During the next quarter century he emerged as a great spokesman and organizer of the church. He became perhaps the most renowned preacher of his day and is credited with converting Augustine of Hippo. He was a highly competent scholar and theologian. He was a hymn writer of some distinction (see *The Hymnal 1940,* 132, 158, and 160). He contributed so much to the design of Christian worship in Milan the rite used there still bears his name, the Ambrosian Rite. He was diligent against heresy, but chastised fellow bishops who allowed heretics to be executed. He was fearless in contending with officials of the Roman state and once even excommunicated the emperor when the latter had perpetrated a vengeful massacre.

Grant to all bishops and pastors the same excellency in preaching and fidelity in ministering your Word as given to your servant Ambrose.

Lucy

Martyr of Sicily

Icon of Purity and Light

The story of Lucy is short and compelling. It typifies the stories which reflect the suffering of the church under the Roman Emperor Diocletian (284-305). This was a period of severe and wide-spread persecution. Lucy was an innocent young maiden of Syracuse, Sicily, who was converted to Christianity and, as a result, gave her dowry to feed the poor and vowed to remain unmarried. This, it is said, so infuriated her fiancé that he reported her to the authorities. She was seized and ordered to be thrown into a brothel. When she resisted, she was slain with a sword. Immediately her story spread and Christians everywhere saw in Lucy a symbol of the innocence and charity of the new order and in her persecutors a symbol of the corruption of the old. Her relics eventually came to rest in Venice where, to this day, gondoliers sing in praise of "Santa Lucia."

Probably because of her name, which means "light" in Latin, a lamp became her symbol and she became the patroness of those with eye diseases. Her feast day falls in the Advent/Christmastide season and her life and witness are often celebrated with reference to "the Light which has come into the world." This is especially true in Scandinavia where she is depicted in radiant baptismal white, with a wreath of candles in her hair.

Some Other Popular Saints

There are many popular saints who, for one reason or another, have never found a place in the official calendar of the Episcopal Church in the United States. Among these are the following, all of whom have Episcopal churches named for them in the United States and all of whom appear in other Anglican calendars. They are presented here simply for purposes of identification.

Agatha *February 5, c.250*

Agatha was a maiden of Catania, Sicily, who was executed by the governmental authorities for her practice of the Christian faith.

Christopher *July 25*

In Greek *christophoros* means "one who bore Christ." In the fourth and fifth centuries churches were sometimes named in honor of the "Christ-bearers": the evangelists and martyrs. In Latin Christendom, *Sancti Christophoroi* was probably misunderstood to be a reference to a "Saint Christopher" and many charming legends grew up around this imaginary saint.

Charles *January 30, 1649*

The second Stuart monarch of England, Charles I, was a pious Christian and a devoted husband and father, but an inept ruler. He was brutally beheaded by Puritan rebels in 1649. Since he had championed the cause of the church against Puritan innovations, he was heralded a martyr by Anglicans and in 1660 a special commemoration of his sacrifice was placed in *The Book of Common Prayer*.

Crispin and Crispinian *October 25*

Legends abound of these great brothers, Crispin and Crispinian, Italian shoemakers who are said to have evangelized Soissons, France, and Faversham in Kent, England. There is no reliable historical record, which, of course, does not mean that they did not exist.

Edward the Confessor *October 13, 1066*

This Anglo-Saxon King of England was highly regarded for his piety, temperance, and generosity to the poor and infirm. He founded Westminister Abbey and there his remains lie in great honor to this day.

Faith *October 6, c.280?*

There seems to have been a martyr of Agen in Aquitaine by the name of Faith, but the evidence is sparse and inconclusive. A number of early churches were named *Sancta Fides*, "Holy Faith," and some of the faithful may have mistaken this for a reference to a Saint Faith. The use of the English word "saint" to mean simply "holy" was not uncommon, e.g. "Saint Saviour." One tradition has it that St. Faith's mother was St. Sophia, an obvious misunderstanding of *Sancta Sophia*, "Holy Wisdom," the name of the great cathedral in Constantinople and of many smaller churches. There was no St. Sophia, no St. Saviour, probably no St. Christopher (see Christopher, above), and possibly no St. Faith.

George *April 23, c.250*

George was a Roman soldier, serving in Palestine, who was converted to Christ and consequently was martyred at Lydda. He typified many such soldiers who witnessed to the faith with their lives and deaths. He is patron of England and of the Anglican cathedral in Jerusalem.

Giles *September 1, c.725*

Giles was a famous hermit who lived in the woods near Arles, France. In the Middle Ages the story of his life was so corrupted by pious legends it is impossible to construct a biography today.

Helena, or Helen

Helena was the Christian mother of Constantine the Great.
She is most famous for having identified many holy places
in Palestine. She lobbied the Imperial government and
succeeded in getting significant funding for the relief of
orphans, widows and the infirm.

Olaf

Olaf was a Norwegian prince who went "a viking" in
England where he was converted and baptized. When
he became King of Norway he imported English priests
to teach the Christian faith to his people. He was killed
in battle, defending crown and country.

Osmund

Osmund came from Normandy to England with William
the Conqueror, whose chancelor he was. But, he is most
famous for his years of service as Bishop of Salisbury
(Sarum). There he oversaw the completion of the mag-
nificent cathedral and the beginning of the Sarum Rite,
the medieval Latin rite which became the basis for *The
Book of Common Prayer*.

Oswald of Worcester

February 28, 992

This cheerful Dane, educated in France, served for thirty years as Bishop of Worcester. He was an unflagging ascetic and a strict but much loved disciplinarian. His good humor and compassion for the unfortunate were said to be unbounded.

Paulinus of York

October 10, 644

Paulinus was an Italian sent from Rome to be the first Roman Catholic bishop of the ancient diocese of York. Anglo-Saxon and Welsh traditions regarding his work there are remarkably different. He eventually had to abandon York and he ended his days as Bishop of Rochester, where an Anglo-Saxon king and the Latin rite were well established.

Sebastian

January 20, c.300

Sebastian was a handsome Gaul and a member of the Roman Emperor's Pretorian Guard. When the authorities discovered that he was a Christian he was sentenced to be shot to death with many small arrows. This failed to kill him, so he was finally bludgeoned to death. He was buried on the Appian Way. His execution became a favorite subject of Christian art.

Swithin, or Swithun

This trusted counselor to two Anglo-Saxon kings was the Bishop of Winchester. Many miracles have been attributed to him and to his shrine in Winchester Cathedral.

Thomas Becket

Thomas was made Archbishop of Canterbury by his friend, King Henry II of England. He engaged in a long and tedious controversy with the King, defending the rights of the church and opposing governmental interference. He was murdered in Canterbury Cathedral by four knights, during Christmastide, a martyr to religious freedom. He is probably the most popular of all English saints. His shrine became the favorite place of pilgrimage in England and his story became one of the most told. (Witness: Tennyson's *Becket*, T.S. Eliot's *Murder in the Cathedral* and Anouilh's *Becket*.)

Thomas More

A leading English humanist, author and Lord High Chancelor, Thomas More rejected King Henry VIII's notorious "Act of Supremacy" which declared that the King was the Supreme Head of the Church of England. For this Thomas was imprisoned in the Tower of London and beheaded. He died defending the liberty of the Church in England. His published works, *Utopia*, *a treatise on the Passion of Christ*, and *Dialogue of Comfort*, probably do not get the reading they deserve today.

A Christian priest named Valentine was martyred on this day on the Flaminian Way near Rome, probably in 269. Later, this day was also associated with another Valentine, the Bishop of Terni, also a martyr of Rome. The custom of sending "valentines" to lovers derives from the pagan feast of Lupercalia, a fertility festival which honored the god Fauna (Pan to the Greeks) and which fell on February 15th.

The best sort of Christian education is knowing a saint, Massey Shepherd once said. Only a few of God's holy people are in official lists. Most have lived relatively quiet lives of self-giving love for God and neighbor. Sometimes they are not much noticed even by those who know them best. But if we search our memories we will come upon them, heroes and heroines of the church who showered nonpossessive love on all who came near them, who did justice, loved kindness and walked humbly with God. These we may remember in our own personal calendars.